Rising in Christ

Meditations on

Living the Resurrection

by Pope John Paul II

To Father Nash
Summer of 2,007

may Charlotte M. Miller
God Bless You on
your journey

theWORD
among us®
press

The Word Among Us Press
9639 Dr. Perry Road
Ijamsville, Maryland 21754
www.wordamongus.org

First published in hardcover in 2004

Cover design: Evelyn Harris
Book design: David Crosson

Made and printed in the United States of America

Library of Congress Cataloging-in-Publication Data

John Paul II, Pope, 1920-
[Selections. English. 2006]
Rising in Christ : meditations on living the resurrection / by Pope John Paul II ;
Jo Garcia-Cobb and Keith E. Cobb, editors.-- 2nd ed.
   p. cm.
Includes bibliographical references.
ISBN 1-59325-071-1 (alk. paper)
1. Jesus Christ--Resurrection--Meditations. 2. Catholic Church--Prayer-books
and devotions--English. I. Garcia-Cobb, Jo. II. Cobb, Keith E., 1947- III. Title.
BT482.J64213 2006
232'.5--dc22
                                    2005032057

Rising in Christ

Meditations on
Living the Resurrection
by Pope John Paul II

Edited by Jo Garcia-Cobb and Keith E. Cobb

the WORD
among us®
press

To our daughter,
Anna Maria

Man who departs endures in those who follow.
Man who follows endures in those departed.
Man endures beyond all coming and going
in himself
and in you.

—Karol Wojtyla
Excerpt from *A Conversation with God Begins*

Table of Contents

Heart ~ To See God Face-to-Face: The Deepest Desire of the Human Spirit ~ "Have Faith in God and Have Faith Also in Me" ~ Knowing Christ in Scripture and in the Breaking of Bread ~ How Christ Overcomes Our Difficulty in Recognizing Him ~ God's Way with Doubting Thomas

Part II: Living the Resurrection

The Apostles Performed "Miracle Signs" ~ Martyrs Proclaim the
Power of Christ's Resurrection

Live in the Joy of the Resurrection

by Pope John Paul II

The Easter event—the bodily resurrection of Christ—pervades the life of the whole church. It gives to Christians everywhere strength at every turn in life. It makes us sensitive to humanity with all its limitations, sufferings, and needs. The resurrection has immense power to liberate, to uplift, to bring about justice, to effect holiness, to cause joy.[1]

In a true sense, joy is the keynote of the Christian message. My wish is that the Christian message may bring joy to all who open their hearts to it. . . . *Faith is our source of joy.* We believe in a God who created us so that we might enjoy human happiness—in some measure on earth, in its fullness in heaven. We are meant to have our human joys: the joy of living, the joy of love and friendship, the joy of work well done. We who are Christians have a further cause for joy: Like Jesus, we know that we are loved by God our Father. This love transforms our lives and fills us with joy. It makes us see that Jesus did not come to lay burdens upon us. He came to teach us what it means to be fully happy and fully human. Therefore, we discover joy when we discover truth—the truth about God our Father, the truth about Jesus our Savior, the truth about the Holy Spirit who lives in our hearts.

We do not pretend that life is all beauty. We are aware of darkness and sin, of poverty and pain. But we know Jesus has conquered sin and passed through his own pain to the glory of the resurrection. And we live in the light of his paschal mystery—the mystery of his death and resurrection. *We are an Easter People and Alleluia is our song!* We are not looking for a shallow joy but rather a joy that comes from faith, that grows through unselfish love, that respects the "fundamental duty of love of neighbor, without which it would be unbecoming to speak of joy" (Paul VI, *Gaudete in Domino*, 1). We realize that joy is demanding; it demands unselfishness; it demands a readiness to say with Mary: "Be it done unto me according to thy word" (Luke 1:38).[2]

We all have been called to accept this joy in our lives. It is given to us again each day in the Eucharist, in which the paschal mystery is renewed: In a sacramental, mystical way the sacrifice of Christ is made present with its culmination in the mystery of the resurrection. The life of grace, which we carry within us, is the life of the risen Christ. Consequently, through grace, a joy beats within us and nothing can take it away. As Jesus promised his disciples: "Your hearts will rejoice, and no one will take your joy away from you" (John 16:22).[3]

Acknowledgments

Our profound gratitude goes to the following people who helped make this book happen: Patricia Mitchell, our editor, who is a joy to work with. Jeff Smith, our publisher, and the rest of The Word Among Us family, for taking on this project. Fr. Joseph Betschart, our former pastor, whose spiritual guidance and insightful homilies made a profound difference in our Easter journey.

Our mothers, Geneva E. Cobb and Remedios D. Garcia, for their prayers and generous gifts of support. Gerry and John Beyer, Lois Lewis, Melody Ashworth, Andrea Mennenbach, Mary Ferrara, and Nokomis Baze for generously helping with the care of our daughter while we were working on this book.

Debra Hampton, our former editor, who helped conceive this book. Rev. William Miller, for his assistance with the Latin and Greek translations in the glossary. Fr. Augustine DeNoble, O.S.B. and Fr. John Cihak, for their editorial comments.

Our parish families, past and present, for being a source of joy and strength: St. Mary's Church, Fairfield, Iowa; Our Lady of the Mountain Church, Ashland, Oregon; St. Mary's Parish, Mt. Angel, Oregon; and the Mt. Angel Abbey and Seminary, St. Benedict, Oregon. Deacon Art Anderson, Teresa and Francis Mottet, Linda Orlin, and Ken and Jessica Malloy, who ushered us into the church with much love and care.

Dear friends, for their encouragement and support during the writing of this book: Madeleine Taylor, Shirley Garcia, Sandy and Ric Morris, Karen and Ed Kerwin, Cal and Monique Baze, Zeny and Clarissa Yance, Lily Ann Suharto,

Ellis and Millie Wilson, Janusz Kiszynski, Sheila Morin, and Paul Steinbroner. For teachers whose lives sowed the seeds of faith in our lives: Sr. Ma. Anthea Raso, M.I.C; Clodualdo de Mundo, Jr. and Dreena del Mundo.

L'Osservatore Romano and the Vatican Web site (www.vatican.va) for publishing the pope's homilies, general audiences, and other speeches, and for permitting their reproduction.

Introduction

For us, the resurrection used to be a religious event of only hazy significance. That changed, however, during the Lenten and Easter seasons of 2003—the result of a personal journey that led us deeply into the Easter experience. The first fruits of this journey have been a peace and joy that continue to grow and deepen as never before. Our journey, which partly involves the writing and editing of this book, owes much of its depth and direction to the life and work of Pope John Paul II, whose enduring witness to the risen Christ has transformed countless lives, including our own. We are happy to share some aspects of our journey in the epilogue of this book.

Throughout the ages, the risen Christ has made himself known through the lives of the people he has transformed. In looking at such lives—such as those of the saints—we see an interior journey that crosses a familiar landscape: the passage from unbelief to faith, from sin to holiness, and ultimately from death to immortality. Scripture and early church writings describe this "Easter passage" as the major turning point in the life of a believer. Whether it takes an instant, as with St. Paul, or occurs over time, as with most people, it is a passage through which one begins a "new life" in Christ. The experience is: "It is no longer I who live, but Christ who lives in me" (Galatians 2:20). As St. Gregory Nazianzen (c. 325–389), early church Father and doctor of the church, strikingly relates of his "first" Easter: "I was crucified with Christ. Today I am glorified with him. Yesterday I died with him; today I am revived with him. Yesterday I was buried with him; today I am resurrected with him."

As we make this Easter passage, Pope John Paul II reminds us that the resurrection, though a historical event, "transcends and stands above history."[1] He explains: "The liturgy of the Easter season reminds us, in various ways, that the mystery of Christ's death and resurrection must become *a daily program of new life* for Jesus' disciples."[2] This book is meant to serve this purpose: to be a prayerful guide to those making their Easter passage so that they can draw from the depths of Easter joy. Such is the joy that comes from knowing what Christ's resurrection means to our lives; from knowing how we, like the apostles, can be empowered by the risen Christ; and from living a new and resurrected life in Christ. As the late Holy Father tells us: "Easter must not remain only on the emotional level or in our memories. It must leave a mark. It must continuously be felt in our lives. Every day, it must encourage us to consistently give Christian witness. Easter is, to the Christian, an invitation to live a 'new life.'"[3] The life and work of Pope John Paul II was a constant witness to the risen Christ, who is at the heart of all his messages. These messages tell the story of God's unbounded love for all people, the love death could not conquer, the love that gives us entry into the life of God himself. *Rising in Christ* is about this love, as the Son of the living God lived it through his death and resurrection, and how he taught us to live the resurrected life.

The selections made for this book span almost twenty-five years of Pope John Paul II's papacy. They include excerpts from the Holy Father's encyclicals, apostolic letters, homilies, *urbi et orbi* messages, *Angelus* reflections, general audiences, and *Regina Caeli* meditations—the tip of the iceberg of his prolific writings. Karol Wojtyla is someone who experienced the risen Christ as an enduring prresence in his own life—as a slave laborer and underground semenarian during WWII, a priest in communist Poland, a poet, a philosopher, a teacher, and "papa" to a spiritual family of over one billion faithful—and so is able to lead us through the Easter passage with great depth and clarity. The manner in which he returned to the house of his Father in 2005 was certainly a witness to his faith in the resurrection. His words are indeed "food for the journey."

Each section and chapter of the book is introduced with a brief personal reflection and a prayer written by the editors: our own personal witness to the transforming power of the risen Christ. We hope that these opening prayers will inspire readers to deeply reflect upon their own Easter passage and be led by the Holy Spirit to share with others the fruits of their reflection.

In a sense, we wish that we had had the benefit of this book years ago in our search for truth. As baptized Christians who, much earlier, had little knowledge of our own religion, we each left the church of our baptism to embrace other religions and spiritual traditions. In looking back at our journeys after our return to Christianity, there are two questions we wish we had asked much earlier in life and pursued with great vigor: "Who *really* is Jesus Christ?" and "What is the significance of the resurrection to our individual lives and to all humanity?" What we have learned from working on *Rising in Christ* has made a profound difference in our lives.

May this book, through the faithful witness of Pope John Paul II, help prepare the way of the risen Lord into your hearts as well. And may the joy of the resurrection be your strength at life's every turn.

Jo Garcia-Cobb and Keith E. Cobb
Mount Angel, Oregon

Part I
Knowing the Resurrection

*I want to know Christ and the power
of his resurrection.*

(*Philippians* 3:10)

Chapter 1

The Resurrection as the Person of Jesus Christ

What did Jesus mean when he said, "I am the way, the truth, and the life" (John 14:6)? This question, which touches the core of the nature of God, is a question that many have pondered throughout the ages. Even the apostles, who walked with Christ, were slow to believe that Jesus himself was not just a teacher of truth, but was himself Truth; that he was not just a way, but was the Way; that he was not just a life-giving presence, but was the Author of Life himself.

By laying down his life in the greatest act of love the world has ever known, and by taking it up again in the resurrection, Jesus gave ultimate proof to all he said and did. The doubts and questions of the disciples gave way to the full realization that they were in the presence of the Lord—God himself, who is one with the Father and the Holy Spirit.

"Lord, as we meditate with the Holy Father on the person of Jesus Christ and what his resurrection means for us, we pray for your grace to fill our hearts and minds with this truth. Put to death everything in us that would prevent the marvelous light of your resurrection from flooding our souls, so that we too may grasp not just rays of truth—but the Truth that leads us to full participation in your very own life."

"I Am"

"*I Am*" (John 8:24). The women went to the tomb; they found it empty and heard the message: He is not here! Why do you seek among the dead him who is alive? He has risen! (c.f. Luke 24:5).

"*I Am.*" Long before, Moses had asked God his Name: "*I am who am,*" came the reply from the burning bush (Exodus 3:14).

"*I Am,*" the name of God, of "Yahweh." And Jesus said to the children of Israel: "*Before Abraham was, I Am*" (John 8:58); and then they tried to stone him.

He also said: "When you have lifted up the Son of man, then you will know that *I Am*" (John 8:28).

Then they lifted up the Son of man on the cross and, when he was already dead, they struck his side with the lance and placed his lifeless body in the tomb. But on the third day, early in the morning, from the empty tomb comes the confirmation: *I Am.*

The life and death of the Son of man are rooted in the immortality of *Him who Is.*[1]

"I Am the Way, the Truth, and the Life"

"*I am the way, the truth, and the life.*" Christ uttered these words at the Last Supper on the day before his Passion and death on the cross. He uttered them to the apostles, who were together with him at the time. Through the apostles he uttered them to everyone—the apostles, and thus, the church had these words to bring to all people and nations . . . to the far corners of the earth. . . .

"*I am the way and the truth and the life. No one comes to the Father but through me*" (John 14:6).

The fullness of time had come for Christ to speak that truth: Time had matured. On the next day, he would embrace his martyrdom and crucifixion—and then the resurrection would follow. And then he, the Everlasting Son, would return to the Father.

Therefore, everyone should know that, *on leaving, he shows us the way;* that by following *him* we go to the Father. No one can go to the Father except through Christ. *He is our way.* There is no other way, there is no other mediator between God and human beings, only he, Jesus Christ.

"I am the way and the life." When he declared that to the apostles, he knew that mortal fear would seize them, that before long, when they would witness his capture, torture, Passion on the cross and, finally, his shameful death, they would be gripped by fear. And that is why he anticipated their fear: "Let not your hearts be troubled" (John 14:1). That is why we recognize that last Passover: the redemptive Passover of the Son to the Father—a Passover, a pasch, which is fulfilled through the sacrifice on the cross. However, let not your hearts be troubled . . . "when I go and prepare a place for you, I will come again" (14:3). In that Passover, Easter, the Redeemer of the world leads us, through his death, to a new revelation of Life on the day of the resurrection: "I will come again"—*I will come, giving proof of the life, which is in me*—a life which overcomes death and puts it to death. . . . That life is in me. I am in this Life. *That Life in me is for you . . .* for you—the Twelve and for everyone, who through your word believes in me. That Life is the final gift of the Everlasting God for mortal man.

"I will come again and will take you to myself, that where I am you may be also" (14:3).

"In my Father's house there are many dwelling places" (John 14:2). Let your hearts not be troubled. May you not be frightened of the earthly finality of death. "Have faith in God and faith in me" (14:1).

"I am the way and the truth and the life. . . . " When, at the Last Supper, he said, "I am the truth," he said that as God from God and light from light because only God "is the truth." At the same time, he said that as a man who . . . is the "witness of faith" (c.f. Revelation 1:5), the entire mystery of God: the whole Truth, which is in God. Any single truth which the created mind grasps is but a portion and reflection of that Truth which is in God.

I am the Truth. As Truth, I am the Way, and I am the Life.

We believe in that Life. On the day of the resurrection, Christ finally confirmed the reality of his entire messianic mission, the entire proclamation of the gospel. The final witness became the measure of all truth.[2]

"What Must I Do to Inherit Eternal Life?"

What must I do so that my life may have value, have meaning? This earnest question comes from the lips of the young man in the gospel in the following form: "What must I do to inherit eternal life?" Is a person who puts the question in this form speaking a language still intelligible to the people of today? Are we not the generation whose horizon of existence is completely filled by the world and temporal progress? We think primarily in earthly categories. If we go beyond the limits of our planet, we do so in order to launch interplanetary flights, transmit signals to the other planets, and send cosmic probes in their direction.

All this has become the content of our modern civilization. Science together with technology has discovered in an incomparable way man's possibilities with regard to matter, and they have also succeeded in dominating the interior world of his thoughts, capacities, tendencies, and passions.

But at the same time it is clear that, when we place ourselves in the presence of Christ, when he becomes the confidant of the questionings of our youth, we cannot put the question differently from how that young man put it: "What must I do to inherit eternal life?" Any other question about the meaning and value of our life would be, in the presence of Christ, insufficient and unessential.

For Christ is not only the "good teacher" who shows the paths of life on earth. He is the witness to that definitive destiny which the human person has in God himself. He is the witness to man's immortality. The gospel which he proclaimed with his lips is definitively sealed by the cross and the resurrection in the paschal mystery. "Christ being raised from the dead will never die again; death no longer has dominion over him." In his resurrection Christ has also become the permanent "sign of contradiction" before all programs incapable of leading man beyond the frontier of death. Indeed, at this frontier they silence all man's questionings about the value and meaning of life. In the face of all these programs, the various ways of looking at the world and the various ideologies, Christ constantly repeats: "I am the resurrection and the life."

And so, dear brothers and dear sisters, if you wish to talk to Christ and to accept all the truth of his testimony, you must on the one hand "love the world"—for God "so loved the world that he gave his only Son"—and at the same time you must acquire interior detachment with regard to all this rich and fascinating reality that makes up "the world." You must make up your mind to ask the question about eternal life. For, the form of this world is passing away, and each of us is subject to this passing. Man is born with the prospect of the day of his death in the dimension of the visible world; at the same time, man, whose interior reason for existence is to go beyond himself, also bears within himself everything whereby he goes beyond the world.

Everything whereby man, in himself, goes beyond the world—though he is rooted in it—is explained by the image and likeness of God which is inscribed in humanity from the beginning. And everything whereby man goes beyond the world not only justifies the question about eternal life but in fact makes it indispensable. This is the question that people have long been asking themselves, not only in the sphere of Christianity but also outside it. You too must find the courage to ask it, like the young man in the gospel. Christianity teaches us to understand temporal existence from the perspective of the kingdom of God, from the perspective of eternal life. Without eternal life, temporal existence, however rich, however highly developed in all aspects, in the end brings man nothing other than the ineluctable necessity of death.[3]

Chapter 2
The Resurrection as History

What does the resurrection mean to our lives and to the life of the world? Throughout all of human history, man has sought to know his ultimate source and destiny—to know God. For his part, God, as we know from personal experience and from divine revelation, has sought to make himself known to man. His love for his creation is written on the heart of every human being and in every fiber of creation. In the fullness of time, the time God saw fit to fully reveal himself, he entered human history and became one of us. He lived on earth, died on the cross and, in his resurrection, revealed to us the full meaning of our existence and the promise of eternal life for those who choose to believe in him.

During the Easter vigil liturgy of the church, we recount God's loving action in human history. As we join the Holy Father in reflecting upon some of the principal stages of salvation history, let us reflect upon our own personal history of salvation—how God has led us, and continues to lead us, from every form of darkness to his eternal light.

"Father in heaven, we thank you for revealing to us the full meaning and purpose of human history through the death and resurrection of your beloved Son. Through this ultimate communication of your love for humanity, we know why

we are here, where we come from, and where we are going. We can now see the history of the human race, as well as our own personal history, as no longer mere blips in the fabric of time and space. Through your death and resurrection, we have found our unique and unrepeatable place in the eternal scheme of things. We have found our place in you."

Abraham's Experience Prefigures Christ's Death and Resurrection

As our hearts return to the beginnings of God's covenant with humanity, we turn our gaze to Abraham, to the place where he heard God's call and responded to it with the obedience of faith . . . a model of unconditional submission to the will of God (c.f. *Nostra Aetate*, 3). "By faith Abraham obeyed when he was called to go out to a place which he was to receive as an inheritance; and he went out, not knowing where he was to go" (Hebrews 11:8). . . . In Abraham's life, which marks the beginning of salvation history, we can already perceive another meaning of the call and the promise. The land, to which human beings, guided by the voice of God, are moving, *does not belong exclusively to the geography of this world.* Abraham, the believer who accepts God's invitation, is someone heading towards a promised land that is not of this world. . . .

By faith Abraham, when he was tested, offered up Isaac, and he who had received the promises was ready to offer up his only son, of whom it was said: "Through Isaac shall your descendants be named" (Hebrews 11: 17-18). *This is the climax of Abraham's faith.* Abraham is tested by that God in whom he had placed his trust, that God from whom he had received the promise about the distant future. . . . He is called, however, to offer in sacrifice to God precisely that Isaac, his only son, on whom his every hope is based, in accordance moreover with the divine promise. How could God's promise to him of numerous descendants come true if Isaac, his only son, were to be offered in sacrifice? . . .

At that humanly tragic moment, when he was ready to inflict the mortal blow on his son, Abraham never stopped believing. Indeed, his faith in God's promise reached its climax. He thought that "God was able to raise men even from the dead." This is what this father, tested humanly speaking beyond all measure, thought. And his faith, his total abandonment to God, did not disappoint him. . . .

All of Abraham's experience appears as an analogy of the saving event of Christ's death and resurrection. This man, placed at the origins of our faith, is part of God's eternal plan. There is a tradition that the place where Abraham was to have sacrificed his own son is the very same place where another father, the eternal Father, would accept the offering of his only-begotten Son, Jesus Christ. Thus Abraham's sacrifice can be seen as a prophetic sign of Christ's sacrifice. St. John writes: "For God so loved the world that he gave his only Son" (John 3:16). The Patriarch Abraham, our father in faith, unknowingly brings all believers, in a certain sense, into God's eternal plan in which the world's redemption is accomplished.[1]

The Passover as the Passage from Death to Life

"The LORD drove the sea back by a strong east wind all night, and made the sea dry land, and the waters were divided. The people of Israel went into the midst of the sea on dry ground, the waters being a wall to them on their right hand and on their left" (Exodus 14:21-22).

The People of God was born from this "baptism" in the Red Sea, when it experienced the powerful hand of the Lord who snatched it from slavery in order to lead it to the yearned-for land of freedom, justice, and peace.

The prophecy of the Book of Exodus is fulfilled today also for us, who are Israelites according to the Spirit, descendants of Abraham because of faith (c.f. Romans 4:16). In his Passover, as the *new Moses,* Christ has made us pass from the slavery of sin to the freedom of the children of God. Having died with Jesus, with him we rise to new life, thanks to the power of his Spirit. His baptism has become our baptism.[2]

From now on, Passover means not only the remembrance of the exodus from the land of slavery and the memory of the passage through the Red Sea: from now on, Passover means *the passage from death to life.*[3]

"*Mors, ero mars tua.*" (O Death, I will be your death). . . . Thus says he who is our Pasch. *Pasch* means "passage." It refers to the passage into life through death, just as, under the Old Covenant, Israel once passed into life through the death of the paschal lamb. Yet, that was only a passage into another life upon this earth: from the slavery of Egypt into the freedom of the Promised Land. The church's pasch signifies the passage into the eternal life that comes from God, and that is life in God. No promised land in this world can guarantee such freedom, such life. . . .[4]

In Christ, sin has ceased to be the mortal abyss for man, the water which engulfs him; *his death has, in effect, become death to sin.* He has caused the life-giving power of the Holy Spirit to descend.[5]

The Resurrection Is the Turning Point in Man's Spiritual History

"When the time had fully come, God sent forth his son, born of woman." With these words of his Letter to the Galatians (4:4), the apostle Paul links together the principal moments which essentially determine the fulfillment of the mystery "predetermined in God" (c.f. Ephesians 1:9). The Son, the Word, One in substance with the Father, becomes man, born of a woman, at "the fullness of time." This event leads to the turning point of man's history on earth, understood as salvation history. It is significant that St. Paul does not call the Mother of Christ by her own name, "Mary," but calls her "woman." This coincides with the words of the *Protoevangelium* in the Book of Genesis (c.f. 3:15). She is that "woman" who is present in the central salvific event which marks the "fullness of time": this event is realized in her and through her.

Thus there begins *the central event, the key event in the history of salvation:* the Lord's paschal mystery. Perhaps it would be worthwhile to reconsider it from the point of view of man's spiritual history, understood in the widest possible sense, and as this history is expressed through the different world religions. Let us recall at this point the words of the Second Vatican Council: "People look to the various religions for answers to those profound mysteries of the human condition which, today, even as in olden times, deeply stir the human heart: What is a human being? What is the meaning and purpose of our life? What is goodness and what is sin? What gives rise to our sorrows, and to what intent? Where lies the path to true happiness? What is the truth about death, judgment, and retribution beyond the grave? What, finally, is that ultimate and unutterable mystery which engulfs our being, and from which we take our origin and towards which we move?" (*Nostra Aetate*, 1) "From ancient times down to the present, there has existed among different peoples a certain perception of that hidden power which is present in the course of things and in the events of human life. At times, indeed, recognition can be found of a Supreme Divinity or even a Supreme Father."

Against the background of this broad panorama, which testifies to the aspirations of the human spirit in search of God—at times as it were "groping its way" (c.f. Acts 17:27)— the "fullness of time" spoken of in Paul's letter emphasizes the response of God himself, "in whom we live and move and have our being" (c.f. 17:28). This is the God who "in many and various ways spoke of old to our fathers by the prophets, but in these last days has spoken to us by a Son" (Hebrews 1:1-2). The sending of this Son, One in substance with the Father, as a man "born of woman," constitutes the culminating and *definitive point of God's self-revelation to humanity*. This self-revelation is salvific in character, as the Second Vatican Council teaches in another passage: "In his goodness and wisdom, God chose to reveal himself and to make known to us the hidden purpose of his will by which through Christ, the Word made flesh, man has access to the Father in the Holy Spirit and comes to share in the divine nature" (*Dei Verbum*, 2).[6]

The Resurrection Is the Fulfillment of Salvation History

The great themes of the holy season of Lent remind us and help us relive from the very beginning the various stages of salvation history. It is a combination of history and mystery, woven by the direct intervention of God in the vicissitudes of his people. This is a people whom he chooses, assists, and guides in the rhythms of covenant, which corresponds to a process of liberation.

However, the fulfillment of this grand and impressive divine plan tends towards a single event. Before it, all the other preceding events assume an aspect of preparation, of foreshadowing, or prefiguring (c.f. Colossians 2:16-17). It is the supreme, unique, and unrepeatable event of the incarnation, immolation, and resurrection of the Son of Man. It is, in a single phrase, the paschal mystery.

From this event the bonds of the new covenant are forged, by which Christ, in virtue of his blood, founds a new People of God, calling them to journey on the paths of history towards total salvation.

In the second chapter of *Lumen Gentium,* the Council recalls that "it has pleased God, however, to make men and women holy and save them not merely as individuals, without any mutual bonds, but by making them into a single people, a people which acknowledges him in truth and serves him in holiness."

In this way one's personal relationship with God is certainly not devalued. On the contrary, its value is increased in commitment to social awareness, which has its very origin in God. Let us listen to some prophetic voices: "Then I will be their God, and they shall be my people" (Jeremiah 31:33); "You will be my people, and I will be your God" (Ezekiel 36:28).

This does not refer to a people in a single historical, geographic, or sociological sense. It refers to a messianic people, a true People of God, that "has for its head Christ. . . . The state of this people is that of the dignity and freedom of the sons of God. . . . Its law is the new commandment to love as Christ loved us. . . . Its destiny is the kingdom of God . . . (and it was) established by Christ as a communion of life, charity, and truth" (*Lumen Gentium*, 9).[7]

Chapter 3

The Resurrection as Mystery

In a religious sense, a mystery is a truth that one can only know by revelation and that transcends intellectual understanding. "Blessed are those who have not seen and yet believe" (John 20:29), Jesus told Thomas, who had to put his finger in his wound in order to believe that he was in the presence of the risen Christ. Blessed are they who can plunge into the timeless truth of the resurrection without relying on their own power to know the truth. Blessed are they who can approach a mystery such as this with humble and contrite hearts. Blessed are they who can question and allow themselves to be led by the risen Christ into the answer that satisfies all of their deepest questions—an encounter with God himself. In reflecting upon the resurrection as mystery, the Holy Father proclaims that this mystery remains deep "in [everyone's] heart, . . . deep in the heart of the world. And from there no one can remove it."[1]

As we join the pope in meditating upon the sacraments of Christian initiation, the Easter season, and the Eucharist as passages into the Easter mystery, let us pray for the grace to behold the infinite riches of this mystery in our own hearts.

"Our Lord and our God, since we cannot witness the event of your resurrection with our senses, our only recourse is to encounter you in our hearts, in the very core of our

being. Help us to pass through the veil of time with the power your sacraments give us. May the great seasons of Lent and Easter be a time of profound purification and transformation for your church. May our participation in your death and resurrection through the sacramental life of your church be an everlasting encounter with your glory, so that we too may say, 'We have seen the risen Lord!'"

The Resurrection Transcends History

While the resurrection is an event that is determined according to time and place, *nevertheless it transcends and stands above history.* No one beheld the event in itself. No one could have been an eyewitness of the event. . . . It is this transhistorical feature of the resurrection that must be especially considered if we are to understand to some extent the mystery of that historical, but also transhistorical event, as we shall see immediately.

Indeed, Christ's resurrection was not simply a return to earthly life, like those whom he had raised from the dead during his public ministry: the daughter of Jairus, the young man of Naim, Lazarus. These facts were miraculous events (and therefore extraordinary), but these persons reacquired, through the power of Jesus, "ordinary" earthly life. At a later time they again died, as St. Augustine frequently observes. In the case of Christ's resurrection, the situation was essentially different. In his risen body *he passed from death to "another" life* beyond time and space. This risen body of Jesus was filled with the power of the Holy Spirit and shared in the divine life of glory. So it can be said of Christ, in the words of St. Paul, that he is the "heavenly man" (1 Corinthians 15:47). . . .

It is true that Jesus, after the resurrection, appeared to his disciples; he spoke to them, had dealings with them, and even ate with them; he invited Thomas to touch him in order to be sure of his identity. However, this real dimension of his entire humanity concealed another life which was now his, and which withdrew him from the "normality" of ordinary earthly life and plunged him in "mystery."[2]

"I live and you will live." What took place on the third day? No one saw the Savior's body return to life, or better, to pass directly from death to a higher life, the life of heaven. His body was filled with the life of the Holy Spirit.

In this way it became a glorified body. It was the same body which had been nailed to the cross, but which now possessed properties superior to those which the human body has in its earthly life. Jesus did not return to an earthly existence after his resurrection: he simply appeared to those who were open to faith. When he appeared, he could move as he chose and enter a room whose doors were locked (c.f. John 20:19). In this way he showed that his true life belonged to the heavenly order.

After appearing for forty days, Jesus left the earth definitively and went up to heaven. From that point on, he began to spread among the human race the divine life which fills his body. He rose for us in order to achieve our salvation and give us a share in his divine life: "I live and you will live," he said (John 14:19).

Before leaving the earth to be established in his heavenly power, Jesus announced the sending of the Holy Spirit. He wants this life of the Holy Spirit, which fills his risen body, to become the life of humanity, so that all may be able to benefit from the fruit of his resurrection.[3]

The Sacraments and Eastertide as Passage into the Paschal Mystery

"This is the day of Christ the Lord!" we sing in the liturgy of Easter Sunday. However, Easter Sunday continues; rather, it is now endless. It is the day of Christ's definitive victory over the devil, over sin, and over death. It is the day which opens onto the temporal cycle the endless perspective of eternal life where the sacrificial Lamb still offers himself continually to the Father for us, for love of us.

For this reason the liturgy celebrates in the octave of Easter the unique day of the pasch. In the mystery of the *ogdoad* (of the octave), as the pastors and teachers of the ancient church admirably explained in their commentaries, the whole mystery of salvation is summarized. In it is included the onward course of time into eternity, of the corruptible into incorruption, of the mortal into immortality. Everything is new, everything is holy, because Christ our Pasch is sacrificed. In this day of the pasch there is anticipated the eternal day of paradise.

These ideas are marvelously expressed in poetic form by the ancient *Stichira* of the Byzantine liturgy which were sung also in Rome in the ninth century in the presence of the pope on Easter Sunday. This year [1988] they were again sung in the Vatican Basilica: "Today a divine pasch has been revealed to us, a new and holy pasch, a mysterious pasch, a most solemn pasch. A pasch, Christ the Redeemer, a great and immaculate pasch, a pasch of the believers. A pasch which opens to us the gates of paradise."

During Eastertide the church turns her thoughts and reflection, and especially her prayer, to contemplate this ineffable mystery. Indeed, she returns there every Sunday of the year, for every Sunday is a little pasch which recalls and presents anew the death and resurrection of Christ. *The pasch, in fact, is not an isolated event, but is linked with our destiny and our salvation.* The pasch is a feast that concerns us and affects us interiorly, because, as St. Paul says: "Christ was put to death for our transgressions and was raised for our justification" (Romans 4:25). Thus Christ's fate becomes ours, his Passion becomes ours, and his resurrection our resurrection.

This stupendous reality is experienced by us believers through the sacraments of Christian initiation. This begins with baptism, which we recall during the Easter vigil. It is the sacrament of rebirth from on high (c.f. John 3:3), the sacrament which reproduces in a mystical way in each believer the Lord's death and, as St. Paul writes: "We were buried therefore with him by baptism into death, so that as Christ was raised from the dead by the glory of the Father, we too might walk in newness of life" (Romans 6:4). Therefore during the Easter vigil we "renew" our baptismal promises.

[The Sacrament of] Confirmation, then, strengthening the bond that unites us to Christ, our Redeemer, makes us his witnesses. Just as the apostles are witnesses of the resurrection and the church lives by their testimony, so likewise Christians are called to live in the light of Easter. Jesus, who breathes the Holy Spirit on the apostles on the very evening of the Sunday of the resurrection, continues to give us his Spirit, whose fullness he has granted to us in the gift of confirmation. . . .

In the Eucharist there is still Jesus who, as in the house of Emmaus, breaks the bread with us, nourishes us with his body and blood which had been sacrificed, stays with us, and transfigures our daily life with his sacramental presence. The

Eucharist unites us to Christ and to our brothers and sisters; it makes us a single family; it makes us forgetful of self in order to give ourselves to others; it makes us think in a practical way of those who suffer, are ill, who lack the necessities of life. It makes us concerned for those who are tried by war, hunger, terrorism, the lack of essential freedoms, among which, in the first place, is the freedom to profess one's faith. Therefore the Byzantine liturgy also contains the chant: "It is the day of the resurrection! Let us irradiate joy for this feast, let us embrace one another, let us accept as brethren even those who hate us, let us pardon all because of the resurrection."

Eastertide should therefore commit us also, as it once did in the case of the disciples of Emmaus, to a renewed journey of faith alongside the risen One, on the way which leads to where the Lord manifests himself in the act of breaking the bread: "Their eyes were opened and they recognized him," as the evangelist Luke tells us (24:31). This season is therefore marked particularly by a greater demand to live more deeply the life of Christ, the life of grace. It is the time in which Christians are called to a greater awareness of the newness and joy, the serenity and seriousness of the Christian life, the demand for its authenticity, fidelity, and consistency. Living the mystery of the risen Christ also requires that we be conformed to him in our way of thinking and acting. St. Paul reminds us of this when he writes to the Colossians: "If you were raised with Christ, seek what is above, where Christ is seated at the right hand of God. Think of what is above, not of what is on earth" (Colossians 3:1-2).[4]

The Eucharistic Meal: Food for Eternal Life

"He who feeds on my flesh and drinks my blood has life eternal" (John 6:54). In instituting the Eucharist on the eve of his death, Christ wanted to give the church a food that would continually nourish it and have it live the same life as the risen One.

Some time before the institution, Jesus had announced this meal, the only one of its kind. In the Jewish religion there were not lacking sacred meals which were eaten in the presence of God and manifested the joy of divine favor. Jesus goes beyond all this: now it is he, in his flesh and blood, who becomes food and drink for mankind. *In the Eucharistic meal, man feeds on God.*

When for the first time Jesus announces this food, he arouses the amazement of his listeners, who do not come to grasp such a high divine plan. Jesus therefore strongly emphasizes the objective truth of his words, affirming the necessity of the Eucharistic meal: "Let me solemnly assure you, if you do not eat the flesh of the Son of Man and drink his blood, you have no life in you" (John 6:53). It is not a question of a purely spiritual meal, in which the expressions "eat the flesh" of Christ and "drink his blood" would be vested with a metaphorical meaning. It is a true meal, as Jesus forcefully defines: "My flesh is real food, and my blood real drink" (6:55).

This food, moreover, is no less necessary to the development of the divine life in the faithful than material food is for the preservation and development of bodily life. *The Eucharist is not a luxury* offered to those who would want to live more intimately united with Christ. It is a necessity of Christian life. This necessity was understood by the disciples since, according to the testimony of the Acts of the

Apostles, in the early times of the church the "breaking of bread"—that is, the Eucharistic meal— was practiced every day in the homes of the faithful "with exultant and sincere hearts" (Acts 2:46).

Guarantee of resurrection. In the promise of the Eucharist, Jesus explains why this food is necessary: "I am the bread of life," he declares (John 6:48). "Just as the Father who has life sent me and I have life because of the Father, so the man who feeds on me will have life because of me" (6:57). The Father is the first source of life: this life he has given to the Son, who in turn communicates it to mankind. He who feeds on Christ in the Eucharist does not have to wait until the hereafter to receive eternal life. He already possesses it on earth, and in it he possesses the guarantee of the resurrection of the body at the end of the world: "He who feeds on my flesh and drinks my blood has life eternal, and I will raise him up on the last day" (6:54).

This guarantee of resurrection comes from the fact that the flesh of the Son of Man given as food *is his body in its glorious risen state.* Those who heard the promise of the Eucharist did not accept this truth: they thought Jesus wanted to [offer] his flesh in the state of its earthly life, and they therefore showed great repugnance for the announced meal. The Master corrects their way of thinking, making it definite that it is a question of the flesh of the Son of Man "ascended to where he was before" (John 6:62), that is, in the triumphant state of his ascension into heaven. This glorious body is filled with the life of the Holy Spirit, and this is why he can sanctify men who feed on it and give them the pledge of eternal glory.

In the Eucharist, therefore, we receive the life of the risen Christ. In fact, when the sacrifice is effected sacramentally on the altar, there is made present not only the mystery of the Savior's Passion and death, but also the mystery of the resurrection, in which the sacrifice finds its crowning. The Eucharistic celebration has us participate in the redemptive offering, but also in the triumphant life of the risen Christ. This is the reason for the atmosphere of joy that characterizes every Eucharistic liturgy. Although commemorating the drama of Calvary, marked at one time by immense sadness, the priest and the faithful rejoice in uniting their offering to Christ's because at the same time they can live the mystery of the resurrection, inseparable from this offering.[5]

The Resurrection Is a Constant Reality in Those Who Accept Its Mystery

Jesus Christ is aware that the end of his earthly mission is approaching: that the moment of leaving the world is approaching. He speaks about it clearly to those closest to him, to the apostles gathered in the Upper Room: "It is to your advantage that I go away" (John 16:7). At the same time he says: "I will not leave you desolate; I will come to you" (14:18) "and your hearts will rejoice" (16:22). So he says: *I am going away . . .* and he says: *I will come to you.*

This going away that is approaching—this end that must arrive: the going away through the Passion, the cross, and death is the beginning of the new coming. It will be manifested on the third day by means of the resurrection of Christ, in the power of the Holy Spirit, and it will always last in all those who, accepting the mystery of the resurrection of

Christ, submit their hearts to the power of this Spirit, whose descent takes place constantly.

This truth is important and fundamental both for each of us . . . and also for every community of the People of God in the church. . . . It is an important and fundamental truth because the full profile of the life, which we have in Jesus Christ, is outlined in it. We live in the profile of his going and, at the same time, of his coming. We live in the power of the Holy Spirit, who brings it about that our human life has its new beginning in the resurrection of Christ and its end in God himself, who knows no limits.[6]

Introduction to Chapters 4 – 6

The Resurrection as a Passage

In the following reflection, which introduces the next three chapters, we join the Holy Father as he elucidates the "paschal meaning of life"—what it means to live in the light of Christ's death and resurrection. All Christians, from the early church until today, are called to make this threefold passage as they live their new life in Christ.

"*Our Lord and our God, help us to live our lives in the great light of your death and resurrection. Help us to rise above our unbelief, our inclinations to sin, and our fear of death. Give us the grace to put our full trust in you as we make our passage with you, through you, and in you, so that we never lose our way in this life as we journey toward eternal life.*"

The Paschal Meaning of Life

"*Pasch*," as we know, means "passing," a word which is interpreted in various ways. First of all, it recalls the historic and adventurous "passing" of the Jewish people led by Moses from the slavery of the Egyptians to the freedom of a nation chosen by God in relation to the coming of the Messiah. Next, it indicates the sacrifice of the lamb slain by the Jews before leaving, and afterwards the perennial annual remembrance of this passover. It also describes Jesus himself, the Messiah, the true Lamb whose sacrifice freed humanity from oppression by sin and determined the "passing" from the Old to the New Testament. Finally, "pasch" signifies Jesus' passing from death to new life. In fact, "pasch" or Easter, in the generally accepted sense, indicates precisely Christ's glorious resurrection, the third day after his death on the cross, as he had foretold.

Passing from unbelief to faith. For the Christian, then, to have the "paschal meaning" of life means first of all *to have a profound and firm conviction that Christ is truly the Son of God,* the Incarnate Word, absolute Truth, the Light of the world.

The evocative ceremonies of the Easter vigil on Holy Saturday, with the symbols of fire, baptismal water, and the solemn singing of the "*Exsultet,*" are meant precisely to point out that Christ is the Light of the world . . . which emphasizes that only Christ, the Redeemer, carries the light of divine revelation, dispels the darkness, and solves the enigma of history. Before the risen Christ the Christian therefore feels courage, zeal, and enthusiasm to proclaim to the whole world the truth: "Repent, and believe in the gospel!"

Passing from sin to holiness. The "paschal meaning" of life consists in a thorough understanding of the saving effects of the redemption, accomplished by Jesus' Passion and death on the cross. This is exactly what Holy Week, with its eloquent rites, wishes to recall, by putting before us the tragic sequence of events from the agony in Gethsemani to the dying cry of Jesus nailed to the cross. . . .

[Jesus'] death on the cross was a sacrifice of expiation; it makes us understand both the gravity of sin as a rebellion against God and a rejection of his love, and the marvelous saving work of Christ which was offered for humanity and which has restored us to grace and therefore to participation in God's Trinitarian life and to the inheritance of eternal happiness. Jesus' Passion and death on the cross give us the true and definitive meaning of life where the redemption is already realized in the perspective of eternity. Just as Christ is risen, so too we will rise in glory, if we have accepted his message and mission.

On Good Friday, let us kneel in prayer before the crucified Christ with St. Paul: "I have been crucified with Christ; it is no longer I who live, but Christ who lives in me; and the life I now live in the flesh I live by faith in the Son of God, who loved me and gave himself for me" (Galatians 2:20).

Passing from death to immortality. Finally, the "paschal meaning" of life also is wonderfully evident in the Holy Thursday Evening Mass of the Lord's Supper, which recalls the institution of the Sacrifice-Sacrament of the Eucharist. Jesus, in his infinite and loving wisdom, wished that the unique and unrepeatable sacrifice of Calvary, the supreme act of adoration and expiation, would remain ever present in history by means of priests and bishops expressly appointed by him for this purpose.

Therefore Holy Thursday reminds us that the life of a Christian must be Eucharistic; the enlightened and consistent Christian cannot do without Mass and Holy Communion, because he knows that he cannot do without the Lord's pasch![1]

The risen Christ is the principle and source of our future resurrection. When he foretold the institution of the Eucharist, Jesus referred to himself as the sacrament of eternal life and of the future resurrection: "He who eats my flesh and drinks my blood has eternal life, and I will raise him up at the last day" (John 6:54). Since his hearers "murmured," Jesus said to them: "Do you take offense at this? Then what if you were to see the Son of man ascending where he was before?" (6:61-62). In this way he indirectly indicated that under the sacramental species of the Eucharist, those who receive it are granted to partake of the body and blood of the glorified Christ.[2]

Chapter 4

From Unbelief to Faith

For those who witnessed the resurrected Christ, unbelief or doubt became unshakable certainty that Jesus was indeed Lord of the universe. "All of us who are called Christians must make this passage from unbelief to faith,"[1] states the Holy Father. "Faith concerns an invisible reality which is beyond sense experience, and surpasses the limits of the human intellect itself. As St. Paul says, it refers to 'what the eye has not seen, and ear has not heard, and what has not entered the human heart,' but what God has prepared for those who love him (c.f. 1 Corinthians 2:9)."[2] As we join the pope in reflecting upon the passage from unbelief to faith, let us ask Jesus to look into our hearts as he looked into the hearts of his first witnesses. May his gaze bring us peace as it frees us of any lingering doubts.

"Our Lord and our God, even before your resurrection, you gave your mother, John the Baptist, and Peter the grace to know and proclaim that you are the Christ, the Son of the living God. We pray that we may know and proclaim this superhuman truth without the trappings of our doubts and questions. For those of us who have shunned you and persecuted your church, we pray for the great light that you sent Paul. Humble us and blind us with your light so that the scales of pride and prejudice may fall from our eyes. For

*those of us who, like Thomas and Philip, doubted and asked
for greater proofs of your divinity even as you stood before
them, we pray that you satisfy all our doubts and questions,
so that our hearts may finally rest in you.*"

God's Work in Peter's Soul

"Blessed are you . . . For flesh and blood has not revealed
this to you, but my Father who is in heaven" (Matthew
16:17). Simon heard these words from Christ's mouth when
he alone answered the question: "Who do men say that the
Son of man is?" (16:13) as follows: "You are the Messiah
(*Christos*), the Son of the living God" (16:16).

The history of Simon, whom Christ began to call Peter, is
centered on this reply. The place in which it was spoken is
a historical place. . . . There Peter's faith was reconfirmed:
"Flesh and blood has not revealed this to you, but my Father
who is in heaven" (Matthew 16:17). Christ hears Peter's confession, which has just been uttered. Christ looks into the soul
of the apostle, who confesses. He rightly speaks of the Father's
work in this soul. The Father's work reaches the intellect, the
will, and the heart, independently of "flesh" and "blood,"
independently of nature and the senses. The Father's work, by
means of the Holy Spirit, reaches the soul of the simple man,
of the fisherman of Galilee. The interior light that comes from
this work finds expression in the words: "You are the Christ,
the Son of the living God." (16:16)

The words are simple. But superhuman truth is expressed
in them. Superhuman, divine truth is expressed with the help
of simple, very simple, words. Such were Mary's words at
the moment of the annunciation. Such were the words of

John the Baptist at the Jordan. Such are the words of Simon in the neighborhood of Caesarea Philippi. . . . By confessing the revealed truth on the divine sonship of his Master, Simon becomes a participant in divine insight, that inscrutable knowledge that the Father has of the Son, as the Son has of the Father. And Christ says: "Blessed are you, Simon Bar-Jona" (Matthew 16:17).

The history of Simon Peter is centered on these words. This blessing was never withdrawn. Just as that confession, which he made then near Caesarea Philippi, was never dimmed in Peter's soul. With it he spent the whole of his life up to his dying day. With it he spent that terrible night of Christ's capture in the garden of Gethsemani; the night of his own weakness, of his greatest weakness, which was shown in his denying the man . . . but which did not destroy his faith in the Son of God. The ordeal of the cross was compensated with the testimony of resurrection, which brought a definitive proof to the confession made in the region of Caesarea Philippi.

Now, with this faith of his in the Son of God, Peter was going towards the mission which the Lord had assigned to him. When, by order of Herod, he found himself in the prison of Jerusalem, chained and condemned to death, it seemed that this mission was to last but little. But Peter was released by the same power by which he had been called. The way marked out for him was still a long one. . . .

At the end of this way, the apostle Peter, the former Simon son of Jona, was here in Rome, here, in this place in which we find ourselves now, under the altar where the Eucharist is being celebrated. His "flesh and blood" were destroyed completely; they were subjected to death. But what the Father had once revealed to him (c.f. Matthew 16:17) survived the death of the flesh. It became the beginning of the eternal meeting with the Master to whom he bore witness up to the end—the beginning of the blessed vision of the Father's Son. And it became also *the unshakable foundation of the faith of the church:* Her stone, the rock. "Blessed are you, Simon Bar-Jona" (16:17).[3]

God's Radical Intervention in Paul's Heart

Saul, persecutor of Christians and of the newborn church, becomes the apostle of that very Christ whose enemy he had been. It happened at the gates of Damascus. Provided with letters from the Sanhedrin in Jerusalem, Saul was on his way to Damascus, intending to arrest the Christians there and bring them to Jerusalem where they would be punished. All of a sudden, he was surprised by a blinding light: "A great light from heaven suddenly shone about me. And I fell to the ground and heard a voice saying to me, 'Saul, Saul, why do you persecute me?' And I answered, 'Who are you Lord?' And he said to me, 'I am Jesus of Nazareth whom you are persecuting" (Acts 22:6-8).

In that instant he realized that all his efforts against Christians were attacks on Jesus Christ. Paul did not know him personally. He felt, in accordance with the Sanhedrin's view, that Jesus' condemnation to death on the cross was certainly just, and he refused to accept what was being said about his resurrection. On approaching Damascus, he found himself face to face with the risen Christ who, as traditional iconography describes very clearly, makes him fall to the ground by an invisible power, blinds him with the splendor that accompanies his appearance, and says: "I am Jesus of Nazareth whom you are persecuting" (Acts 22:8).

In saying this, the risen Christ identifies himself with his disciples; he identifies himself with the church. Paul instantly understands all this. It makes a dazzling impression on his soul and becomes the source of all the inspiration that he was later to express in his letters. One could say that at that moment, he received the full light of the gospel through revelation and was converted.

Moved to the depths of his heart, Paul asked: *"What shall I do, Lord?"* And the Lord answered him: "Rise, and go into Damascus, and there you will be told all that is appointed for you to do" (Acts 22:10). Thus it happened. In Damascus, Ananias, a faithful observer of the law who had become a Christian, went to him. He said to him, "Brother Saul, receive your sight." Paul instantly recovered his sight. Ananias added, "The God of our fathers appointed you to know his will, to see the Just One, and to hear a voice from his mouth; for you will be a witness for him to all men of what you have seen and heard . . . Rise and be baptized, and wash away your sins, calling on his name" (22:14-16).

Previously, Ananias had received the following instructions from the Lord: "Go, for he is a chosen instrument of mine to carry my name before the Gentiles and kings and the sons of Israel: for I will show him how much he must suffer for the sake of my name" (Acts 9:15-16).

Thus from being Christ's persecutor, Paul became his apostle. All those who saw and heard him were amazed: "Is not this the man who made havoc in Jerusalem of those who called on this name? And he has come here for this purpose, to bring them bound before the chief priests" (Acts 9:21).[4]

If every conversion, or *metanoia*, is the work of divine grace—that is, God's direct and radical intervention in the heart of man—Paul's is so in the highest degree. . . . This experience, which transforms Saul into Paul the apostle, once more teaches us how great events, which determine the life of the church, spring from the grace of the Lord, who intervenes in our personal life and in our hearts and shapes the church's history how and when he wills.[5]

To See God Face-to-Face: The Deepest Desire of the Human Spirit

As man strives to know God, to perceive his face and experience his presence, God turns towards man to reveal his own life. The Second Vatican Council dwells at length on the importance of God's intervention in the world. It explains that through divine revelation, "God chose to show forth and communicate himself and the eternal decisions of his will regarding the salvation of men" (*Dei Verbum*, 6).

At the same time the merciful and loving God who communicates himself through revelation still remains for man an inscrutable mystery. And man, the pilgrim of the Absolute, continues throughout his life to seek the face of God. But at the end of the pilgrimage of faith, man comes to the "Father's house," and being in this "house" means seeing God "face to face" (1 Corinthians 13:12).

This seeing God "face to face" is the deepest desire of the human spirit. How eloquent in this context are the words of the apostle Philip when he says to Jesus: "Lord, show us the Father, and we shall be satisfied" (John 14:8). Those words are indeed eloquent because they bear witness to the deepest thirst and desire of the human spirit.[6]

It is almost like hearing the question which has always tormented man, needful of certainty and security, desirous of meeting with God. Jesus answers with firm authority: "Whoever has seen me has seen the Father. Do you not believe that I am in the Father and the Father is in me? The words I speak are not spoken of myself; it is the Father who lives in me accomplishing his works. Believe me that I am in the Father and the Father is in me" (John 14:9-11).[7]

Jesus is the revelation of the Father; he explains to the world what the Father is like, not because he is the Father but because *he is one with the Father* in the communion of divine life. In the words of Jesus: "I am in the Father and the Father in me" (John 14:11); man no longer has to search all alone for God. In partnership with Christ, man discovers God and he discovers him in Christ.[8]

"Have Faith in God and Have Faith Also in Me"

When Philip asks that the disciples be shown the Father, Jesus replies with absolute clarity: "Whoever has seen me has seen the Father. How can you say, 'Show us the Father'? Do you not believe that I am in the Father and the Father is in me? The words that I speak to you I do not speak on my own. The Father who dwells in me is doing his works. Believe me that I am in the Father and the Father is in me, or else, believe because of the works themselves" (John 14:9-11).

One cannot escape the grip which this statement of Jesus has on human intelligence unless one begins from an *a priori* prejudice against the divine. To those who admit the Father, and indeed sincerely seek him, Jesus shows himself and says: "Behold, the Father is in me!"

If motives of credibility be needed, Jesus appeals to his works, to all that he did before the eyes of the disciples and the whole people. These were holy and frequently miraculous works which served as a confirmation of his truth. For this reason he is worthy of belief. Jesus says so not only in the circle of the apostles, but also before the entire people. In fact we read that on the day following his triumphal entry into Jerusalem, the large crowd who had come for the paschal celebrations were discussing the figure of the Christ, and generally they did not believe in Jesus, "although he had performed so many signs in their presence" (John 12:37).

At a certain point, "Jesus cried out, 'Whoever believes in me believes not only in me but also in the one who sent me, and whoever sees me sees the one who sent me" (John 12:44-45). It can therefore be said that Jesus Christ identifies himself with God as the object of the faith asked of and proposed to his followers. He explains to them: "What I say, I say as the Father told me" (12:50). This is an obvious allusion to the eternal utterance whereby the Father generates the Word-Son in the Trinitarian life.

This faith, linked to the works and words of Jesus, becomes a "logical consequence" for those who honestly listen to Jesus, observe his works, and reflect on his words. But it is also the presupposition and indispensable condition which Jesus demands of those who wish to become his disciples or benefit from his divine power.[9]

Knowing Christ in Scripture and in the Breaking of Bread

After his resurrection the Lord appeared to [the two disciples from Emmaus] on their way home, but they failed to recognize him. He explained to them how the Easter festival of the new covenant was prophesied in the events and writings of the Old Testament. . . . Numerous statements in the Old Testament prophesy what happened at the Last Supper and on Golgotha. These prophecies would not have been fulfilled, however, if the events of Easter had not taken place in Jerusalem at the time and in the manner predetermined by God. Yet the disciples of Jesus did not immediately recognize the true meaning and the deeper truth of the dramatic and moving events with their Master during the Jewish Passover. They were slow to believe all that the prophets had announced (c.f. Luke 24:25). This truth was so hard for them to accept, seeing as they were used to a different interpretation of the holy Scripture. Why should the Messiah have to suffer, be condemned, die on the cross, and be despised and ridiculed like an outcast? Thus, at first they were as if blinded, discouraged and sad, paralyzed as it were. . . .

Christ himself interpreted to the disciples of Emmaus the deeper meaning of what had happened as being connected with the divine plan of salvation as indicated in the Word of the holy Scripture: "Beginning then with Moses and all the prophets, he interpreted to them every passage of Scripture which referred to him" (Luke 24:27). At all times God has moved people through the word of his revelation and renewed the church. . . .

This encounter on the road from Jerusalem to Emmaus is so significant: not just in connection with the events of Easter then, but for always, for all time, and for us. On this road the disciples learned from Jesus how to read the holy Scriptures anew and to discover in them prophetic testimony of him, a prophecy of his coming, his gospel, and his mission of salvation. By this means the Lord prepared his disciples who were to be his witnesses. . . .

The encounter on the road to Emmaus is also of great importance, since after his death on the cross Jesus promised his disciples that he would remain with them. He remained with them in spite of Good Friday or, perhaps, we could say precisely because of Good Friday, and he will always remain with his church in accordance with his promise: "I will not leave you orphaned; I will come back to you" (John 14:18). Christ is not just he who was. More than that, *he is he who is.* He was present on the road to Emmaus. He *is* present on all the roads of the world on which his disciples have traveled through the generations and the centuries.[10]

How Christ Overcomes Our Difficulty in Recognizing Him

Some characteristics of the meetings [between Jesus and his disciples following the resurrection] are in a certain way typical examples of the spiritual situations which so often arise in personal relationships with Christ when people feel called or "visited" by him.

Above all, there is an initial difficulty in recognizing Christ on the part of those who meet him, as can be seen in the case of Mary Magdalene (John 20:14-16) and of the disciples on the road to Emmaus (Luke 24:16). There is a certain element of fear in his presence. He is loved, he is sought, but when found, there is a certain hesitation.

In the case of Mary Magdalene (John 20:14-16), of the disciples on the road to Emmaus (Luke 24:26-31), and similarly in the case of the other disciples (c.f. 24:25-48), Jesus gradually led them to recognize him and to believe in him. It is a sign of Christ's patient pedagogy in revealing himself to people, in attracting them, in converting them, in leading them to the knowledge of the riches of his heart and to salvation.

It is interesting to analyze the psychological process that the various meetings give us a glimpse of. The disciples experience a certain difficulty not only in recognizing the truth of the resurrection, but also the identity of the One who stands before them. He appears as the same and yet as different: a "transformed" Christ. It is not easy for them to identify him immediately. Yes, they perceive that it is Jesus, but at the same time they feel that he is not in the same condition as he was before, and in his presence they are seized with reverence and fear.

When they realize with his help that it is not a case of someone different, but of himself transformed, there is released in them a new capacity for discovery, understanding, charity, and faith. It is like an awakening of faith: "Did not our hearts burn within us while he talked to us on the road, while he opened to us the scriptures?" (Luke 24:32). "My Lord and my God!" (John 20:28). "I have seen the Lord!" (20:18). Then they began to understand the event of the cross in an absolutely new light: the mystery of Christ's suffering and death was seen to end in the glory of new life! This will be one of the principal elements of the announcement of salvation brought by the apostles from the very beginning to the Jewish people and gradually to all nations.[11]

God's Way with Doubting Thomas

"Blessed are they who have not seen and yet believe" (John 20:29). These words of the risen Christ resound from the Upper Room in Jerusalem towards the far-off future. Through the centuries and generations they will reach to the end of time.

That truly was the "day the LORD has made" (c.f. Psalm 118:24): the day on which Christ, crucified and laid in the tomb, rose. On the same day he appeared to the apostles gathered in the Upper Room. They saw him with their own eyes. . . . One of the Twelve, Thomas, was not with the apostles when Christ came into their midst. And when all the others told him about the meeting with the Master, he did not want to believe. The testimony of the apostles' words was not enough for him. He asked to see. "Unless I see . . . unless I place my finger . . . I will not believe" (John 20:25).

But faith is not sight. "Faith comes from what is heard, and what is heard comes through the word of Christ" (Romans 10:17).

Still, Christ gave Thomas the opportunity to see, by going to the Upper Room expressly for him eight days later on the octave of the resurrection. Thomas was able to be convinced with his very eyes, that he who had been crucified, who had really died and had been laid in the sepulcher was alive. In view of the testimony his own eyes gave, before the testimony of all his senses—denial gave way to affirmation. . . . He said it all in a few words, and expressed all that the fact of the resurrection contains within itself: *"My Lord and my God!"* (John 20:28). No one has proclaimed the truth about Christ so openly, and so unhesitatingly.

One can also say that Thomas' faith surpassed his unbelief by quite a margin. It became not only certainty, *but a real enlightening.* On the one hand, Thomas demonstrates how hard it is for a person to accept the truth of the resurrection; on the other, he attests that the resurrection is an important and decisive testimony to God's omnipotence. It is a key event among the workings of God in human history and in the history of all created things. . . .

The church's faith originates in the apostles, eyewitnesses, but it is maintained and developed through generations *as the fruit of hearing:* hearing their testimony, hearing the Word of God himself, proclaimed by the church, which is built upon the foundation of the apostles and prophets.[12]

Chapter 5
From Sin to Holiness

We live in an era where many have lost the sense of how sin defiles our inmost self and builds barriers that divide us from God and from one another. Yet sin causes countless vows and hearts to be broken and countless sufferings to be inflicted. The immense weight of our sins burdens our hearts and our world. "We all are in need of repentance," the Holy Father reminds us. "We all have the possibility of conversion." As we join the pope in his meditations on the Easter passage from sin to holiness, let us pray for "the radical change of mentality which leads a person to abandon the path of selfishness and travel the road of assent to God's truth and love." [1]

"Our Lord and our God, you know our hearts more than we do; you know our transgressions against you and our neighbors more than we do. We pray that your Holy Spirit, who searches the depths of our hearts, will reveal to us every-thing that encumbers us. Help us to sincerely repent of our sins and to make the passage from sin to holiness, so that we may know the joy of a pure heart, the joy of doing only your will. Lord, give us the grace to die, once and for all, to our sins, to bury our old selves, and to live a new life in you."

God's Mercy Alone Can Free Us from Sin

The psalmist [David] is fully aware that the "joy of salvation" flows from liberation from sin: "For I know my transgressions, and my sin is ever before me" (Psalm 51:3).

Sin is a stain. It defiles the person in his most intimate spiritual life. Therefore the psalmist cries out: "Wash me thoroughly from my iniquity, and cleanse me from my sin" (Psalm 51:2). He is fully aware that sin is an evil which encumbers the person's soul and weighs on his conscience. Therefore he says: "For I know my transgressions, and my sin is ever before me." He also knows that sin, this evil which burdens and encumbers the person's soul, is an obstacle placed between the person and God. "Against thee, thee only, have I sinned, and done that which is evil in thy sight" (51:4).

The image of sin thus presented is full of meaning. In it both dimensions which determine the measure of guilt meet: on one side the human being with his conscience sensitive to good and evil; on the other side the greatness and holiness of God. Man lives in his presence. From the very beginning, God is he who questions man about the truth of his conscience. Adam, "Where are you?" (Genesis 3:9). He also is the only One to whom man can reveal the whole truth *by confessing it to him.* However, God is not only the judge who knows all. He is at the same time the only One to whom man can cry: "Blot out my transgressions," blot them out according to thy abundant mercy (c.f. Psalm 51:1). "Blot out" means: "See to it that this evil, which encumbers my soul and weighs upon my conscience, be wiped out! You alone can do it! You alone!"

You alone can "wipe out," because you alone can create. In me, man, sin is unable to disappear if you will not create me anew. . . .

It is necessary that each of us, every member of contemporary society, reread these words of the ancient psalm. They are simple, profound, penetrating. They are capable of revealing again and again the special world which man bears within himself and which contemporary man—perhaps especially Western man with his unidimensional civilization—has, in a certain sense, pushed away from himself. He has lost the sense of it.

With this he has also lost the fundamental dimension of his human identity, his Christian identity. In trying to "erase" sin—the reality of sin—from his conscience, he has also lost the great goods which this reality makes accessible: the full dimension of his human identity, real sensitivity of conscience and, in the last analysis, that unique dignity which derives from being in the presence of God, from being in the ray of the light which emanates from his "face."[2]

"What Shall We Do?"

After recording Peter's first discourse on the day of Pentecost, the author of Acts informs us that those present "were cut to the heart" (Acts 2:37). They are eloquent words which indicate the action of the Holy Spirit in the souls of those who heard from Peter the first apostolic preaching of his witness concerning Christ crucified and risen, and his explanation of the extraordinary events which had taken place that day. In particular, that first public presentation of the paschal mystery reached the very core of the expectations of the people of the Old Covenant, when Peter said: "God has made both Lord and Christ this Jesus whom you crucified" (2:36).

The same Holy Spirit who had descended upon the apostles was now at work in the hearts of those who heard the apostolic preaching. Peter's words touched their hearts, awakening in them "a conviction of their sinfulness," the beginning of conversion.

Filled with remorse, " . . . they said to Peter and the rest of the apostles, 'Brethren, what shall we do?'" (Acts 2:37). The question, "What shall we do?" shows their readiness of will. It was the interior good predisposition of Peter's listeners that, on hearing his words, made them aware that it was necessary to change their lives. . . .

"Repent." Peter himself now replies to the question of those present. It is a very simple reply: . . . "Repent" (2:38). It was with this exhortation that Jesus had begun his messianic mission (c.f. Mark 1:15). Now Peter repeats it on the day of Pentecost, in the power of the Spirit of Christ who descended on him and on the other apostles. . . .

"Repent," on the lips of Peter means: change from the rejection of Christ to faith in the risen One. The crucifixion had been the definitive expression of the rejection of Christ, sealed by an ignominious death on Golgotha. Now Peter exhorts those who crucified Jesus to have faith in the risen One. . . . The exhortation to conversion implies above all faith in Christ the Redeemer. Indeed, the resurrection is the revelation of that divine power which, by means of Christ's crucifixion and death, effects man's redemption and his liberation from sin. . . .

"Be baptized." Following faithfully what Christ had laid down (c.f. Mark 16:16; Matthew 28:19), Peter calls not only for "repentance" but also for baptism in Christ's name "for the forgiveness of . . . sins" (Acts 2:38). In fact, the apostles on the day of Pentecost were "baptized in the Holy Spirit" (c.f. 2:4). Therefore, in passing on the faith in Christ the Redeemer, they urge people to be baptized, for baptism is the first sacrament of this faith. Since it effects the forgiveness of sins, the faith should find in baptism its own sacramental expression so that man may share in the gift of the Holy Spirit.

This, we may say, is the ordinary way of conversion and grace. Other ways are not excluded for "the Spirit blows where it wills" (c.f. John 3:8) and can accomplish the work of salvation by sanctifying man apart from the sacrament, when its reception is not possible. It is the mystery of the meeting between divine grace and the human soul. . . .

By virtue of Christ's victorious love, the church also is born in the sacramental baptism through the work of the Holy Spirit on the day of Pentecost, when the first conversions to Christ took place. We read in fact that "those who received his word (that is, the truth contained in Peter's words) were baptized, and there were added that day about three thousand souls" (Acts 2:41); that is, "they were added" to those who had been previously "baptized in the Holy Spirit," the apostles. Having been baptized "with water and the Holy Spirit," they become the community "of the adopted sons of God" (Romans 8:15). As "sons in the Son" (c.f. Ephesians 1:5) they become "one" in the bond of a new brotherhood. Through the action of the Holy Spirit they become the church of Christ.[3]

"A New Spirit I Will Put within You"

Having come in search of Christ, Nicodemus [a member of the Sanhedrin] declares his faith: "Rabbi, we know that you are a teacher come from God; for no one can do these signs that you do, unless God is with him" (John 3:2). Jesus answers him: "Truly, truly, I say to you, *unless one is born anew,* he cannot see the kingdom of God" (3:3). Nicodemus asks him: "How can a man be born when he is old? Can he enter a second time into his mother's womb and be born?" (3:4). Jesus replies: "Truly, truly, I say to you, unless one is born of water and the Spirit, he cannot enter the kingdom of God. That which is born of the flesh is flesh, and that which is born of the Spirit is spirit" (3:5-6).

A spiritual birth. Jesus makes Nicodemus pass from things visible to things invisible. Each one of us is born of man and woman, of a father and a mother; this birth is the point of departure of our whole existence. Nicodemus is thinking in terms of this natural event. On the other hand, Christ came into the world to reveal a different birth, the spiritual birth. . . . "Unless one is born of water and the Spirit, he cannot enter the kingdom of God" (John 3:5). Thus, in order to enter the kingdom, a person must be born anew, not according to the flesh but according to the Spirit. *Baptism is precisely the sacrament of this birth.* The apostle Paul gives a profound explanation of this in the passage from the Letter to the Romans which we have heard: "Do you not know that all of us who have been baptized into Christ Jesus were baptized into his death? We were buried therefore with him by baptism into death, so that as Christ was raised from the dead by the glory of the Father, we too might walk in newness of life" (6:3-4). The apostle gives us here the meaning of this new birth; he shows why the Sacrament of Baptism takes place by immersion into water. This is not a merely symbolic immersion into the life of God. Baptism is the concrete and effective sign of immersion into Christ's death and resurrection. . . .

Dead to sin, alive to God. Everyone who receives this baptism *is given a share in Christ's resurrection.* St. Paul returns often to this theme, which sums up the essence of the true meaning of baptism. He writes: "If we have been united with him in a death like his, we shall certainly be united in with him in a resurrection like his" (Romans 6:5). And also: "We know that our old self is crucified with him so that the sinful body might be destroyed, and we might no longer be enslaved to sin. For he who has died is freed from sin. But if we have died with Christ, we believe that we shall also live with him. For we know that Christ being raised from the dead will never die again; death no longer has dominion over him. The death he died he died to sin, once for all, but the life he lives he lives to God. So you also must consider yourselves dead to sin and alive to God in Christ Jesus" (6:6-11). With Paul, . . . you say to the world: Our hope is steadfast; through Christ we live for God.[4]

What the Sacrament of Baptism Does to Us

Dear friends, do you know what the Sacrament of Baptism does to you? *God acknowledges you as his children and transforms your existence into a story of love with him.* He conforms you to Christ so that you will be able to fulfill your personal vocation. He has come to make a pact with you, and he offers you his peace. Live from now on as children of the light who know that they are reconciled by the cross of the Savior! . . .

Baptism makes you share in the church's life. Baptism—"mystery and hope of the world to come" (St. Cyril of Jerusalem, *Procatechesis,* 10, 12)—is the most beautiful of God's gifts, inviting us to become disciples of the Lord. It brings us into intimacy with God, into the life of the Trinity, from this day forward and on into eternity. It is a grace given to the sinner, a grace which purifies us from sin and opens to us a new future. It is a bath which washes and regenerates. It is an anointing which conforms us to Christ, Priest, Prophet, and King. It is an enlightenment which illumines our path and gives it full meaning. It is a garment of strength and perfection. Dressed in white on the day of our baptism, as we shall be on the last day, we are called to preserve every day its bright splendor and to discover it anew, through forgiveness, prayer, and Christian living. Baptism is the sign that God has joined us on our journey, that he makes our existence more beautiful, and that he transforms our history into a history of holiness.[5]

What the Sacrament of Reconciliation Does to Us

We know that in order to communicate the fruits of his Passion and death to people, the risen Christ conferred on the apostles the power to forgive sins: "Whose sins you forgive are forgiven them, and whose sins you retain are retained" (John 20:23). In the church the priests, as heirs of the mission and power of the apostles, forgive sins in Christ's name. However, we can say that in the Sacrament of Reconciliation, the priest's specific ministry does not exclude but rather includes the exercise of the "common priesthood" of the faithful, who confess their sins and ask for pardon under the influence of the Holy Spirit who converts them intimately through the grace of Christ the Redeemer. In affirming this role of the faithful, St. Thomas cites the famous words of St. Augustine: "He who created you without you will not justify you without you."[6]

The words of our Savior [c.f. John 20:23] remind us of the *fundamental gift of our redemption: the gift of having our sins forgiven and of being reconciled with God.* Remission of sin is a completely free and undeserved gift, a newness of life which we could never earn. God grants it to us out of his mercy. As Saint Paul wrote: "It is all God's work. It was God who reconciled us to himself through Christ and gave us the work of handing on this reconciliation" (2 Corinthians 5:18).

There is no sin which cannot be forgiven, if we approach the throne of mercy with humble and contrite hearts. No evil is more powerful than the infinite mercy of God. In becoming man, Jesus entered completely into our human experience, even to the point of suffering the final and most cruel effect of the power of sin—death on a cross. He really became one like us in all things but sin. But evil with all its power did not win. By dying, Christ destroyed our death; by rising, he restored our life; by his wounds we are healed and our sins are forgiven. For this reason, when the Lord appeared to his disciples after the resurrection, he showed them his hands and his side. He wanted them to see that the victory had been won; to see that he, the risen Christ, had transformed the marks of sin and death into symbols of hope and life. . . .

The church is, by her nature, always reconciling, handing on to others the gift that she herself has received, the gift of having been forgiven and made one with God. She does this in many ways, but especially through the sacraments, and in particular through Penance.

In this consoling sacrament she leads each of the faithful individually to Christ, and through the church's ministry, Christ himself gives forgiveness, strength, and mercy. Through this highly personal sacrament, Christ continues to meet the men and women of our time. He restores wholeness where there was division, he communicates light where darkness reigned, and he gives a hope and a joy which the world could never give. Through this sacrament the church proclaims to the world the infinite riches of God's mercy, that mercy which has broken down barriers which divided us from God and from one another.[7]

Chapter 6
From Death to Immortality

Ever since death entered our world because of sin, our existence in time has lost its grounding in eternity. We have lost clear sight of our immortality and our heavenly home with God. Yet, the Holy Father reminds us that while "the human existence each of us has received from our parents ends in bodily death, the life received from God in Jesus Christ has no end. The life of God knows no death! In God is the fullness of life."[1] As we join the pope in reflecting upon God's promise of eternal life and the resurrection of the body, let us pray that we will always live our earthly lives as a response to God's infinite love for us. May his love dwell in us and surround us as we make our own passage into eternal life.

"Our Lord and our God, for so long we feared, and could only speculate what might happen after our death. We are eternally grateful that you came, gave us the 'words of eternal life,' and opened for us the way to life everlasting through your own resurrection. Lord, help us to face our own death with confidence and peace. Turn our fears into joy, and our doubts into faith in our own resurrection. Give us a firm resolve and hope that we will spend our eternal lives with you in heaven."

The Risen Christ Conquers Death

"Do not be afraid. I am the first and the last, the one who lives" (Revelation 1:17-18). . . . "Do not be afraid!" When on the island of Patmos Jesus addresses this exhortation to John, he reveals his victory over the many fears that accompany man in his earthly existence and especially when he is faced with suffering and death. The fear of death also concerns the great unknown which it represents. Could it be a total annihilation of the human being? Do not the severe words "For you are dust, and to dust you shall return" (c.f. Genesis 3:19) fully express the harsh reality of death? Thus man has serious reasons to feel afraid when he faces the mystery of death.

Contemporary civilization does all it can to distract human attention from the inescapable reality of death and tries to induce man to live as though death did not exist. And this is expressed practically in the attempt to turn man's conscience away from God: to make him live as though God did not exist! But the reality of death is obvious. It is impossible to silence it; it is impossible to dispel the fear associated with it.

Man fears death just as he fears judgment and punishment. And this fear has a saving value. It should not be eliminated in man. When Christ says: "Do not be afraid!" he wants to respond to the deepest source of the human being's existential fear. What he means is: Do not fear evil, since in my resurrection good has shown itself stronger than evil. My gospel is victorious truth. Life and death met on Calvary in a stupendous combat, and life proved victorious: "*Dux vitae mortuus regnat vivus!*"; "Once I was dead, but now I am alive for ever and ever" (Revelation 1:18).[2]

The Promise of Eternal Life

The life which the Son of God came to give to human beings cannot be reduced to mere existence in time. The life which was always "in him" and which is the "light of men" (John 1:4) consists in being begotten of God and sharing in the fullness of his love: "To all who received him, who believed in his name, he gave power to become children of God; who were born, not of blood nor of the will of the flesh nor of the will of man, but of God" (1:12-13).

Sometimes Jesus refers to this life which he came to give simply as "life," and he presents being born of God as a necessary condition if man is to attain the end for which God has created him: "Unless one is born anew, he cannot see the kingdom of God" (John 3:3). To give this life is the real object of Jesus' mission: He is the one who "comes down from heaven, and gives life to the world" (6:33). Thus can he truly say: "He who follows me . . . will have the light of life" (8:12).

At other times, Jesus speaks of "eternal life." Here the adjective does more than merely evoke a perspective which is beyond time. The life which Jesus promises and gives is "eternal" because it is a full participation in the life of the "Eternal One." Whoever believes in Jesus and enters into communion with him has eternal life (c.f. John 3:15; 6:40), because he hears from Jesus the only words which reveal and communicate to his existence the fullness of life. These are the "words of eternal life" which Peter acknowledges in his confession of faith: "Lord, to whom shall we go? You have the words of eternal life; and we have believed, and have come to know, that you are the Holy One of God" (6:68-69).

Jesus himself, addressing the Father in the great priestly prayer, declares what eternal life consists in: "This is eternal life, that they may know you the only true God, and Jesus Christ whom you have sent" (John 17:3). To know God and his Son is to accept the mystery of the loving communion of the Father, the Son, and the Holy Spirit into one's own life, which even now is open to eternal life because it shares in the life of God.

Eternal life is therefore the life of God himself and at the same time the life of the children of God. . . . Here the Christian truth about life becomes most sublime. The dignity of this life is linked not only to its beginning, to the fact that it comes from God, but also to its final end, to its destiny of fellowship with God in knowledge and love of him. . . .

Immediate consequences arise from this for human life in its earthly state, in which, for that matter, eternal life already springs forth and begins to grow. Although man instinctively loves life because it is a good, this love will find further inspiration and strength, and new breadth and depth, in the divine dimensions of this good. Similarly, the love which every human being has for life cannot be reduced simply to a desire to have sufficient space for self-expression and for entering into relationships with others; rather, it develops in a joyous awareness that life can become the "place" where God manifests himself, where we meet him and enter into communion with him. The life which Jesus gives in no way lessens the value of our existence in time; it takes it and directs it to its final destiny: "I am the resurrection and the life . . . whoever lives and believes in me shall never die" (John 11:25-26).[3]

Earthly Life Is Our Passing to Life in God

The church, a witness to the life of Christ . . . is also a witness of hope: of that gospel hope which finds its source in Christ. Indeed, in the Pastoral Constitution (*Gaudium et Spes,* 45), Vatican II says of Christ: "The Lord is the goal of human history . . . the center of mankind, the joy of all hearts and the fulfillment of all human aspirations." In this text the Council quotes the words of Paul VI, who said in an address that Christ is "the focal point of the desires of history and civilization." As we see, the hope which the church witnesses to has vast dimensions; we can even say it is immense.

It is primarily a question of hope for eternal life. This hope corresponds to the desire for immortality which the human person has in his heart in virtue of the soul's spiritual nature. The church preaches that earthly life is the "passing" to another life: to life in God, where "there shall be no more death" (Revelation 21:4). Because of Christ, who as St. Paul says is "the firstborn from the dead" (Colossians 1:18; c.f. 1 Corinthians 15:20), because of his resurrection, human beings can live in expectation of the eternal life proclaimed and brought by him.

It is a question of hope for happiness in God. We are all called to this happiness, as the command of Christ reveals to us: "Go into the whole world and proclaim the gospel to every creature" (Mark 16:15). On another occasion Jesus assured his disciples that "in my Father's house there are many dwelling places" (John 14:2), and that he was leaving them on earth and going to heaven to "prepare a place for you . . . so that where I am you also may be" (14:3).

It is a question of hope in being with Christ "in the Father's house" after death. The apostle Paul was full of this hope, to the point of saying: "I long to depart this life and be with Christ," and "that is far better" (Philippians 1:23). "We are courageous," he also wrote, "and we would rather leave the body and go home to the Lord" (2 Corinthians 5:8).

Christian hope also assures us that the "exile in the body" will not last and that our hope in the Lord will be fumed with the resurrection of the body at the end of the world. Jesus gives us this certitude; he relates it to the Eucharist: "Whoever eats my flesh and drinks my blood has eternal life, and I will raise him on the last day" (John 6:54). It is a true and proper resurrection of the body, with the full reintegration of individual persons into the new life of heaven, and not a reincarnation understood as a return to life on the same earth in different bodies. In the revelation which Christ preached and to which the church gives witness, the hope of resurrection is placed in the context of "a new heaven and a new earth" (Revelation 21:1), in which the "new life" which men share with the incarnate Word will find its full realization.[4]

Our Future Resurrection

The risen Christ is the principle and source of a new life for everyone. When he foretold the institution of the Eucharist, Jesus referred to himself as the sacrament of eternal life and of the future resurrection: "He who eats my flesh and drinks my blood *has eternal life,* and I will raise him up *at the last day* (John 6:54). Since his hearers "murmured," Jesus said to them: "Do you take offense at this? Then what if you were to see the Son of man ascending where he was before?" (6:61-62). In this way he indirectly indicated that under the sacramental species of the Eucharist, those who receive it are granted to partake of the body and blood of the glorified Christ.

St. Paul, too, emphasizes the connection between Christ's resurrection and ours, especially in his first Letter to the Corinthians where he writes: *"Christ has been raised from the dead, the first fruits of those who have fallen asleep . . .* for as in

Adam all die, so also in Christ shall all be made alive" (15:20, 22). "For this perishable nature must put on the imperishable, and this mortal nature must put on immortality. When the perishable puts on the imperishable, and the mortal puts on immortality, then shall come to pass the saying that is written: 'Death is swallowed up in victory'" (15:53-54). "Thanks be to God, who gives us the victory through our Lord Jesus Christ" (15:57).

The definitive victory over death, already won by Christ, is shared by him with humanity in the measure in which it receives the fruits of redemption. It is a process of admission to the "new life," to the "eternal life" which will last until the end of time. Thanks to this process, there is being formed down the centuries a new humanity, the people of the redeemed, gathered in the church, the true community of the resurrection. At the final moment of history, all shall rise again, and those who belong to Christ will have the fullness of life in glory, in the definitive realization of the community of those redeemed by Christ, "so that God may be everything to every one" (1 Corinthians 15:28).

The resurrection of the body. The apostle also teaches that the redemptive process, concluding with the resurrection of the dead, will take place in a sphere of indescribable spirituality, which transcends the power of human comprehension and operation. If, on the one hand, he writes: "Flesh and blood cannot inherit the kingdom of God, nor does the perishable inherit the imperishable" (1 Corinthians 15:50)—and it is the recognition of our natural incapacity for the new life—on the other hand, in the Letter to the Romans, he thus reassures the believers: "If the Spirit of him who raised Jesus from the dead dwells in you, he who raised Christ Jesus from the dead will give life to your mortal bodies also through his Spirit who dwells in you" (8:11). It is a mysterious process of spiritualization which, at the moment of the resurrection, will affect also the bodies, through the power of that same Holy Spirit who brought about Christ's resurrection.

Undoubtedly it is a reality which escapes our capacity of rational understanding and demonstration, and therefore it is an object of our faith based on the word of God which, through St. Paul's teaching, enables us to penetrate the mystery which transcends all limits of space and time: "The first man, Adam, became a living being; the last Adam became a life-giving spirit" (1 Corinthians 15:45). "Just as we have borne the image of the man of dust, we shall also bear the image of the man of heaven" (15:49).

In expectation of that final transcendent fulfillment, the risen Christ dwells in the hearts of his disciples and followers as a source of sanctification in the Holy Spirit, a source of divine life and divine Sonship, a source of future resurrection.

This certainly leads St. Paul to say in the Letter to the Galatians: "I have been crucified with Christ; it is no longer I who live, *but Christ who lives in me.* The life I now live in the flesh I live by faith in the Son of God, who loved me and gave himself for me" (2:20). Every Christian also, like the apostle, while still living in the flesh (c.f. Romans 7:5), lives a life already spiritualized though faith (c.f. 2 Corinthians 10:3), because the living Christ, the risen Christ, has become as it were the subject of all his actions: *Christ lives in me* (c.f. Romans 8:2, 10-11; Philippians 1:21; Colossians 3:3). It is the life in the Holy Spirit.

This certainly sustained the apostle, as it can and should sustain every Christian amid the toils and sufferings of the present life, as Paul recommended to his disciple Timothy in a passage of one of his letters with which we wish to put the seal—for our instruction and consolation—on our reflection on Christ's resurrection: "Remember Jesus Christ," he writes, "risen from the dead, descended from David, as preached in my gospel . . . Therefore I endure everything for the sake of the elect, that they may obtain the salvation which in Christ Jesus goes with eternal glory. The saying is sure: If we have died with him, we shall also live with him; if we endure, we shall also reign with him; if we deny him, he also will deny us; if we are faithless, he remains faithful, for he cannot deny himself. . ." (2 Timothy 2:8, 10-13).

"Remember that Jesus Christ is risen from the dead": these words of the apostle are the key of our hope for the true life in time and in eternity.[5]

The Joy That Knows No End

There is yet another book to which the liturgy of the Easter season turns; it is the Book of the Apocalypse of Saint John. It is the book of the "last end times." The resurrection of Christ historically gave rise to the apostolic preaching of the gospel and to the church, and at the same time it was the beginning of the "ultimate fulfillment" of everything in Christ. Therefore, especially in the Easter season, the church renews its consciousness of existing in the eschatological dimension of definitive fulfillment.

In the second reading of today's Mass [Revelation 21:1-5], the ultimate fulfillment of things is presented as the moment of the supreme and final joy of the holy city, the church, the

New Jerusalem. She has been created and willed by God's inmost being for this ultimate and eternal moment. She then descends from heaven, from God, because she is the fruit of divine love and initiative, the fruit of the grace which will crown all human history. She is "like a bride adorned for her husband," for in the definitive moment, the covenant will be fulfilled in the church and love will be brought to its perfection, to its fullness in her. All the tears shed throughout her history, like all the tears of people brought about by evil, by guilt, and by malice, will disappear because God himself, "God-with-them," will put an end to weeping since he himself will be the perfect joy of every person. The marvelous page of the Apocalypse tells us that, in God's plan, man is destined for this fullness of joy which knows no end, when he will be freed once and for all as though for a new creation. "I make all things new." These are the words which "the one seated upon the throne" in John's vision in the Apocalypse pronounced in today's liturgy.

We are the pilgrim church. We are on the way towards the heavenly Jerusalem, towards that final "new heavens and new earth" which come from God together with the crucified and risen Christ.

The way towards that which "is new" in Christ invites us to pass by way of the commandment of love. It too, in fact, is a new commandment. "I give you a new commandment, that you love one another as I have loved you."

Let us accept this commandment. Let us renew its power in us. Let us respond to the multiple demands it places on us. Let us do everything possible to carry it out in our life.

In this way the Easter mystery of Jesus Christ will constantly fill reality, all of reality, even that normal, everyday reality which is nevertheless always "new," new in the power of Christ's cross and resurrection.

Thus we will be "his people" and he will be "God-with-us" (c.f. Revelation 21:3).[6]

The Assumption of Mary Is a Sharing in Christ's Resurrection

At her assumption, Mary was "taken up to life"— body and soul. She is already a part of "the first fruits" (1 Corinthians 15:20) of our Savior's redemptive death and resurrection. The Son took his human life from her; in return he gave her the fullness of communion in divine life. She is the only other being in whom the mystery has already been completely accomplished. In Mary the final victory of life over death is already a reality. And, as the Second Vatican Council teaches: "In the most holy Virgin the church has already reached the perfection whereby she exists without spot or wrinkle" (*Lumen Gentium*, 65). In and through the church we too have hope of an inheritance which is imperishable, undefiled, and unfading, kept in heaven for us" (c.f. 1 Peter 1:4).[7]

"*A woman clothed with the sun.*" The church applies to Mary these words from the Revelation of St. John. In a certain sense, they tell us the end of the story of the "woman clothed with the sun": they speak to us of Mary assumed into heaven.

The assumption of Mary is a special sharing in Christ's resurrection. In today's liturgy [on the Feast of the Assumption], St. Paul emphasizes this truth, announcing the joy for the victory over death achieved by Christ through his resurrection. "For he must reign until he has put all his enemies under his feet. The last enemy to be destroyed is death" (1 Corinthians

15:25-26). Victory over death, which became evident on the day of Christ's resurrection, today concerns his mother in a very special way. If death has no power over him—that is, over the Son—neither has it any more power over his mother, that is, over her who gave him earthly life.

In his first Letter to the Corinthians, St. Paul as it were makes a profound comment on the mystery of the assumption. He writes thus: "Christ has been raised from the dead, the first fruits of those who have fallen asleep. For as by a man came death, by a man has come also the resurrection of the dead. For as in Adam all die, so also in Christ shall all be made alive. But each in his own order: *Christ, the first fruits,* then at his coming *those who belong to Christ"* (15:20-23). Mary is the first among "those who belong to Christ." In the mystery of the assumption, Mary is the first to receive the glory; the assumption represents, as it were, the culmination of the Easter mystery.

Christ rose again, defeating death, the result of original sin, and with his victory he embraces all those who accept his resurrection with faith: first of all, his mother, freed from the inheritance of original sin by her Son's redemptive death on the cross. Today Christ embraces Mary, immaculate from her conception, receiving her into heaven in her glorified body, as if to hasten for her the day of his glorious return to earth, the day of the universal resurrection awaited by humanity. *The assumption into heaven is like a great anticipation of the ultimate fulfillment of everything in God,* in conformity with what the apostle writes: "Then comes the end, when he [Christ] delivers the kingdom to God the Father that God may be everything to everyone" (1 Corinthians 15:24, 28). Is not God everything in her, the Immaculate Mother of the Redeemer?[8]

Part II

Living the Resurrection

It is no longer I who live,
but Christ who lives in me;
and the life I now live in the flesh
I live by faith in the Son of God,
who loved me and
gave himself for me.

(*Galatians* 2:20)

Introduction to Chapters 7 – 9
How the Resurrection Empowered the Apostles

How did a few ordinary men who had exhibited fear, ignorance, and uncertainty become the enlightened preachers, miracle workers, and builders of God's kingdom on earth? By conquering death, Christ laid to rest any uncertainty they may have harbored about his claim that he was the Son of the living God. Any remaining doubts vanished when the apostles received the Holy Spirit on Pentecost.

During our Easter passage, the Holy Spirit awakens us to the fact that to be part of Christ's body commits us to the same calling that he had for his apostles—to follow him, wherever he may lead us. This is our greatest privilege as well as our greatest challenge. The hope and power that flow from Christ's resurrection also make this calling our greatest joy. Like the apostles, when we follow Jesus, he transforms us and empowers us so that we can accomplish whatever it is that he calls us to do.

In the next three chapters, the Holy Father reflects on the miracle of Pentecost. As we meditate with him, let us pray for a fresh outpouring of the Holy Spirit in our own lives so that we may experience new life in Jesus Christ. We also pray for the vision to see the life of the church as Christ's own life, flowing into and blessing the whole world.

"Our Lord and our God, lead us as we trace the footsteps of your apostles, for these very footsteps have become ours to follow. We pray that the power and new life that flow from your resurrection will transform our lives. Even though we don't always see the path you have set before us, help us to never be afraid. May the faith of the apostles be our guiding light as your resurrection and the coming of the Holy Spirit in our hearts enable us to continue building your kingdom in faithfulness and in truth."

Chapter 7

Preparing for the Coming of the Holy Spirit

In preparing for the coming of the Holy Spirit on Pentecost, the apostles with one accord devoted themselves to prayer, making themselves completely available to God's work in their lives. From being with the Lord in his flesh and blood, they now had to receive God in Spirit. To encounter God's presence in this way, they had to grow much larger than their individual selves by becoming the church he had called them to be. As we join the Holy Father in his meditations on the apostles' prayerful preparation for the coming of the Holy Spirit, let us pray for the intercession of Mary and all the saints who were in the Upper Room, that we would be open to the Spirit's work in our own lives.

"Holy Spirit, we pray that we may be in a constant state of preparation for your coming, for we need you at every turn in our journey. Help us to find the time each day to empty ourselves of everything that might prevent us from receiving you. Help us to create an 'upper room' in our hearts, in our homes, and wherever we may be that is always open to you. Set our hearts on fire with your love. May the church be the one heart through which your Spirit flows to the entire world."

"I Am Going Away and I Will Come Back to You"

On the eve of his Passion, in the Upper Room at Jerusalem, Jesus announced to the apostles the day of his departure to the Father, which was close at hand. "I am going away. . . . I am going to the Father. . . . The Father is greater than I" (John 14:28).

We are drawing near to the time of the ascension of Christ; that is why the church repeats these words for us. Jesus' departure filled the hearts of the apostles with sadness—with sadness and confusion. However, he says to them: "Do not let your hearts be troubled or afraid. . . . I am going away and I will come back to you" (John 14:27-28).[1]

After the resurrection, on the fortieth day, Christ will leave the apostles and return to the Father. This final departure is at the same time the condition for a further presence, which will last from generation to generation, according to Christ's own words: "I am with you always, to the close of the age" (Matthew 28:20).

"I am with you" means: I am with the church built on you, *and I come always in the power of the Holy Spirit.* This coming takes many forms: in the words of the gospel, in the sacraments, especially in the Eucharist, in the mysterious indwelling in the heart through grace. . . .

"I go away, and I will come to you." I will come to you in the power of the Holy Spirit. Christ promises: "The Counselor, the Holy Spirit, whom the Father will send in my name, he will teach you all things, and bring to your remembrance all that I have said to you" (John 14:26). In presenting today these words spoken by Jesus in the Upper Room on the day before his Passion, the liturgy turns our thoughts to the forthcoming mysteries of the Lord's ascension and Pentecost. The

apostles have already received the Holy Spirit in the evening of Easter Day, when the risen One came among them in the Upper Room, showed them the wounds in his hands and his side, and said to them: *"Receive the Holy Spirit"* (20:22).

What took place inwardly must now take place in the midst of the people gathered in Jerusalem for the feast of Pentecost. Jesus will no longer be with his apostles in the Upper Room, but the coming of the Holy Spirit will enable Christ to begin working with new force in them and through them: working as truth and love.

The Counselor, the Holy Spirit, will teach the apostles and the church all that Christ himself told them, until the end of the world. He will see to it that Jesus' teaching, his truth, will abide without end in the church; that the Word, one with the Father in his divinity, will continue to unite people to one another, from generation to generation, in that truth and love which he revealed by his first coming into the world.[2]

This second coming of Christ is going to begin with the descent of the Holy Spirit: "The Advocate, the Holy Spirit that the Father will send in my name—he will teach you everything and remind you of all that I told you" (John 14:26).

Beginning with the day of the ascension, the church, following the example of the apostles, prepares for the coming of the Holy Spirit on the day of Pentecost. The apostles persevered that whole time in prayer with Mary, the Mother of Christ, in the Upper Room.[3]

Your Sorrow Will Turn into Joy

The joy of which Jesus spoke to his disciples on that day before his Passion is also at hand: "Your sorrow will turn into joy" (John 16:20). It will be the joy for the church's birth.

Her sadness over Christ's departure will be changed into his joy when, on Pentecost, the apostles experience that it is the strength of the Spirit of Truth that enables them to witness to the risen Christ, over and above every human consideration and the totality of human weakness.

With the coming of the Holy Spirit the age of the church begins in the history of mankind; the fullness of time, begun on this earth with Christ, conceived by the Holy Spirit and born of the Virgin whose name was Mary, continues to mature in the church.

The message of the Cenacle contains a great mystery. "If I do not go away, the Counselor will not come to you; but if I go, I will send him to you" (John 16:7). These are key words. These words reveal the Trinitarian economy by which the inscrutable God-Father, Son and Holy Spirit operates in time. . . . "I came from the Father and have come into the world; again I am leaving the world and going to the Father" (16:28). "I am leaving the world," even though I am not separating myself from the world. I will remain in it through the Holy Spirit. I will remain in it by the truth of the gospel, through the Eucharist and the church; through the Word and the sacraments; through the grace of divine Sonship; through faith, hope, and charity.

"I am leaving the world"—but I am not separating myself from the world. I will never separate myself from man for all ages. I will lead him to the Father, to the Father's house. Regardless of all the resistance and objection that come from sin throughout the history of the world, I will lead man to the Father.[4]

The First Church Community in Prayer

We read in the Acts of the Apostles that the disciples "then [that is, after the risen Lord's ascension into heaven] returned to Jerusalem. . . . When they entered the city they went to the Upper Room where they were staying, Peter and John and James and Andrew, Philip and Thomas, Bartholomew and Matthew, James son of Alphaeus, Simon the Zealot, and Judas son of James. All these devoted themselves with one accord to prayer, together with some women, and Mary the Mother of Jesus, and his brothers" (Acts 1:12-14). This is the first image of that community, the *communio ecclesialis,* which, we see, Acts describes in a detailed way.

It was a community gathered by the will of Jesus himself, who, at the time he was returning to the Father, ordered his disciples to remain united in expectation of the other event he had announced: "I am sending the promise of my Father upon you; but stay in the city until you are clothed with power from on high" (Luke 24:49).

The evangelist Luke, who was also the author of the Acts of the Apostles, introduces us to that first community of the church in Jerusalem by reminding us of Jesus' own exhortation: "And eating together with them, he enjoined them not to depart from Jerusalem, but to wait for 'the promise of the Father about which you have heard me speak; for John baptized with water, but in a few days you will be baptized with the Holy Spirit'" (Acts 1:4).

These texts show that this first church community, which was to be revealed in broad daylight on the day of Pentecost by the coming of the Holy Spirit, results from an order of Jesus himself, who gave the church her own "form," so to speak. This last text reveals a detail which merits attention: Jesus made this arrangement while "eating together with them" (Acts 1:4). When he would return to the Father, the Eucharist would become for all time the expression of the church's communion, in which Christ is sacramentally present. At this meal in Jerusalem, Jesus was visibly present as the risen Lord, who celebrated with his friends the feast of the Bridegroom who came back among them for awhile.

After Christ's ascension, the little community continued its life. We read especially: "All these [the apostles] devoted themselves with one accord to prayer, together with some women, and Mary the Mother of Jesus, and his brothers" (Acts 1:14). The first image of the church is that of a community which is devoted to prayer. All were praying for the gift of the Holy Spirit who had been promised them by Christ even before his Passion, and again, before his ascension into heaven.

Prayer—prayer in common—is the basic feature of that "communion" at the time when the church began, and so it will always be. This is evidenced in every century—and today as well—by prayer in common, particularly liturgical prayer, in our churches, religious communities and, may God increasingly grant us this grace, in Christian families. . . .

Luke emphasizes the "unanimity" (*homothymadon*) of this prayer. This fact highlights the communal meaning of the prayer. The prayer of the early community—as would always be the case in the church—expresses and serves this spiritual "communion," and at the same time it creates, deepens, and strengthens it. In this communion of prayer, the differences and divisions which come from other material and spiritual factors are overcome: prayer produces the community's spiritual unity.[5]

Chapter 8

How the Holy Spirit Moved
through the Apostles

The Holy Spirit works in mysterious, wondrous ways. He can come like a gentle dove or a mighty wind. He can speak through tongues and set our souls on fire for God. When the Holy Spirit descended upon the apostles, they were altogether transformed; they became miracle workers like their Master, and their fears were banished. Their unity and their love for one another, as well as their love for their enemies, became the greatest wonder of all. Many willed to see their death, but neither death nor time had the power to dim their witness. As we join the pope in his meditations on the Holy Spirit's work in giving birth to the church, let us welcome the Spirit's mighty yet gentle work in us, as we are born into new life.

"O Holy Spirit, we praise and thank you for ceaselessly directing the work of the church from its birth to the end of time, and for keeping it united in love amid great diversity. We pray that you will always keep our minds and our hearts anchored in the certainty that you are with us, and that you will guide, defend, and comfort the church at all times, especially in times of great trial. May we fully use the gifts that you give us to build and strengthen your kingdom on earth. May your work in us and through us bear the same lasting fruit that the apostles' work has borne for the risen Christ."

The Spirit of Truth Will Make You Witnesses

Veni Creator Spiritus! "The earth is full of your Spirit, Lord." This is what the church exclaims as she celebrates the Solemnity of Pentecost, which closes the Easter season focused on Christ's death and resurrection.

After the resurrection, Christ appeared to the apostles several times (c.f. Acts 1:3), strengthening their faith and preparing them to begin the great evangelizing mission which was definitively passed on to them at the time of his ascension into heaven. These were the last words Jesus spoke on earth to his apostles: "Go into all the world" (Mark 16:15). "Make disciples of all nations, baptizing them in the name of the Father and of the Son and of the Holy Spirit, teaching them to observe all that I have commanded you; and lo, I am with you always, to the close of the age" (Matthew 28:19-20). . . .

Power from the Holy Spirit. On the Solemnity of Pentecost there occurred the extraordinary event described in the Acts of the Apostles, which marks the birth of the church. "Suddenly a sound came from heaven like the rush of a mighty wind, and it filled all the house where they were sitting. And there appeared to them tongues as of fire, distributed and resting on each one of them. And they were all filled with the Holy Spirit and began to speak in other tongues, as the Spirit gave them utterance" (2:2-4). These extraordinary phenomena attracted the attention of the Israelites and the proselytes present in Jerusalem for the feast of Pentecost. They were amazed at that rush of wind and still more at hearing the apostles speak in different tongues. Coming from many parts of the world, they heard these Galileans each speaking in his own language: "We hear them telling in our own tongues the mighty works of God" (2:11).

In the Acts of the Apostles, St. Luke describes the extraordinary manifestation of the Holy Spirit at Pentecost as a communication of the very vitality of God who gives himself to men. This divine gift is also *light and power: light,* to proclaim the gospel, the truth revealed by God; *power,* to infuse the courage of witnessing to the faith, which the apostles begin at that very moment. . . .

The witness of the Spirit of truth must become one with that of the apostles, thus fusing the divine and human witness into one saving reality. From this fusion flows the work of evangelization, begun on the day of Pentecost and entrusted to the church as her task and mission down the ages.[1]

The Apostles Could Not Be Silent about the Resurrection

When, in celebrating the Eucharist, the church proclaims Christ's resurrection, she does so by virtue of the testimony of the apostles who personally saw their Master alive again. Their eyewitness account is the most important source of faith for the church, which proclaims Christ's resurrection as an event that really happened, the foundation of faith and a reason for hope to all those seeking salvation. . . .

The apostles, once again taken before the tribunal of the Sanhedrin, again received a severe reprimand from the high priest: "We gave you strict orders to stop teaching in that name. Yet you have filled Jerusalem with your teaching and want to bring this man's blood upon us" (Acts 5:28). But Peter and the apostles reply simply yet firmly: "We must obey God rather than men" (5:29); we must, that is, obey what God commands us, what he entrusts to us as his word, rather than what we are ordered to do by the Sanhedrin.

The apostles, who with their own eyes saw Christ after the resurrection, could not be silent about their extraordinary experience. If he showed himself to them, he did it so that the truth of his resurrection would reach all men through their qualified witness. Jesus' resurrection was the new beginning of God's intervention in the history of the chosen people. In proclaiming Christ's resurrection every day during the celebration of the Eucharist, the church reconnects with this new beginning: "We proclaim your resurrection."[2]

The Spirit Directs the Church's Mission

The mission of the church, like that of Jesus, is God's work or, as Luke often puts it, the work of the Spirit. After the resurrection and ascension of Jesus, the apostles have a powerful experience which completely transforms them: the experience of Pentecost. The coming of the Holy Spirit makes them witnesses and prophets (c.f. Acts 1:8; 2:17-18). It fills them with a serene courage which impels them to pass on to others their experience of Jesus and the hope which motivates them. The Spirit gives them the ability to bear witness to Jesus with "boldness" (4:31).

When the first evangelizers go down from Jerusalem, the Spirit becomes even more of a "guide," helping them to choose both those to whom they are to go and the places to which their missionary journey is to take them. The working of the Spirit is manifested particularly in the impetus given to the mission which, in accordance with Christ's words, spreads out from Jerusalem to all of Judea and Samaria, and to the farthest ends of the earth.

The Acts of the Apostles records six summaries of the "missionary discourses" which were addressed to the Jews during the church's infancy (c.f. Acts 2:22-39; 3:12-26; 4:8-12; 5:29-32; 10:34-43; 13:16-41). These model speeches, delivered by Peter and by Paul, proclaim Jesus and invite those listening to "be converted"—that is, to accept Jesus in faith and to let themselves be transformed in him by the Spirit.[3]

The Apostles' Certainty That the Holy Spirit Was with Them

The entire Acts of the Apostles is a grand description of the Holy Spirit's work at the beginning of the church which, as we read, "was being built up and was making steady progress in the fear of the Lord; at the same time it enjoyed the increased consolation of the Holy Spirit" (Acts 9:31). We know that there were internal difficulties and persecutions, and there were the first martyrs. But the apostles were certain that the Holy Spirit was there to guide them. This awareness of theirs would in some way be formalized in the concluding decision of the Council of Jerusalem, whose resolutions began with the words: "It is the decision of the Holy Spirit, and ours too . . ." (15:28). In this way the community gave evidence of its own awareness of being moved by the action of the Holy Spirit.[4]

It was the Spirit-Comforter promised by Jesus who sustained the apostles and the other disciples of Christ in the first trials and sufferings, and continued to grant the church his comfort during periods of peace and calm as well. This peace depended on him, as did the growth of individuals and communities in the gospel truth. That is how it has always been throughout the centuries.[5]

The Risen Christ Delivers Peter and Paul from All Their Fears

"I sought the LORD, and he answered me, and delivered me from all my fears" (Psalm 34:4). Yes. The Lord delivered me from all my fears. In the context of the readings for today's liturgy [on the Solemnity of Saints Peter and Paul], these words lead us above all to think of that mortal fear experienced by Peter and, together with him, by the whole church at Jerusalem when the apostle was imprisoned by Herod Agrippa I, "intending after the Passover to bring him out to the people" (Acts 12:4).

Without a doubt, this was one of the critical moments at the very beginning of the life of the apostolic church. All the more so since Herod had already "killed James the brother of John with the sword" (Acts 12:2). These were moments of great trial for Peter and the little Christian community at Jerusalem!

Therefore it was not strange that, while Peter was being held in prison and the guard had been especially reinforced, *prayer was lifted up to God unceasingly by the church for him* (c.f. Acts 12:4-5). And the church's prayer is heard. Peter, miraculously led out of the prison, where he had been guarded by four pickets of soldiers, in a certain sense makes the words of the psalmist his own: "The Lord delivered me from all my fears."

Judging by the unfolding of events in the gospel, Simon Peter was not a pusillanimous man. Indeed, he shows a certain vehemence, as when he unsheathes his sword to defend his Master in the Garden of Gethsemani. Yet he also had moments of downfall, witnessed to by the night in Gethsemani and Jesus' arrest, when Peter denied him. He was not present during the *via crucis* nor on Calvary. Without a doubt, the events of Good Friday provoked dejection and fear in the hearts of Peter and the apostles—fear of what had already taken place and of what might happen in its wake.

It is difficult to describe the emotional state in which Peter and the apostles lived after Christ's crucifixion. It is certain that the day of the resurrection brought a radical change: The Lord truly delivered them from all their fears, showing himself to them that same night in the Upper Room.

From fear to love. The fear that had implanted itself in Peter's heart due to the terrible trials of the preceding days had yet not succeeded in destroying his love for Christ. The Lord had delivered him from all his fears through love. Still, we know that Peter was no longer so sure as he had been of his love for the Redeemer. To the question: "Do you love me?" he answered by appealing to what Christ himself could read in his heart (c.f. John 21:17). Yet, Christ also knew his downfalls, his triple denial.

Continuing to follow the course of events recorded in the Acts of the Apostles, we can see that the definitive deliverance from fear came on the day of Pentecost. This is revealed by the behavior of all the apostles. Listening to the words Peter addresses to the inhabitants of Jerusalem on that day: "The Lord delivered me from all my fears," an organic link exists between that day and the day of his martyrdom, which took place in Rome. During that period, Peter appears as a man delivered from all his fears by the power of God: by the power of the Holy Spirit.

This power of God gave shape to the apostolic mission of Peter already proclaimed and conferred upon him by Christ with the words: "You are Peter, and on this rock I will build my church" (Matthew 16:18). This divine power transformed the man. It enabled him to overcome weaknesses and fears. The Lord delivered him from all his fears and confirmed him in that particular service of charity which is the feeding of his sheep. . . .

Paul's liberating moment. Now let us turn our attention to the figure of the apostle Paul, who, like Peter, was transformed by the divine power, but in another way. Without a doubt, Saul of Tarsus was a human personality different from the fisherman of Galilee: He was first a bitter enemy of the "name of Christ," and then he became his most ardent apostle.

In a different way he experienced the power of the Lord acting upon him. In a different way—completely different—he participated in the same paschal experience that Peter and the apostles had first lived through. One could say that the Pasch came to Saul together with Pentecost and transformed him immediately into Paul.

He experienced a greater fear, then, but this was a "liberating" fear. Perhaps we know less of those personality traits of Paul that would permit us to distinguish his maturation from fear to courage, than we do in the case of Peter.

Nonetheless, he too gives us a testimony similar to Peter's: "The Lord stood by me and gave me strength . . . so I was rescued from the lion's mouth. The Lord will rescue me from every evil and save me . . ." (2 Timothy 4:17, 18).

The source of the spiritual strength of the Apostle of the Gentiles, the source of his great vigor, is the Lord: it is Christ crucified and risen, who works through the Spirit of truth. Paul of Tarsus gives transparent witness to this in many places and circumstances. . . .

The testimony of the holy apostles Peter and Paul in a certain sense repeats to everyone, everywhere, with the same simplicity and humanity, but also with the same firmness as in Nero's day: "I sought the LORD, and he answered me, and delivered me from all my fears" (Psalm 33:4).[6]

One in Heart and Mind through the Holy Spirit

The unity desired by Christ found at the time of the church's beginning a fulfillment worthy of being recorded: "The community of believers were of one heart and one mind" (Acts 4:32). . . .

The gospel text documents the importance of fraternal charity as the soul of the community, and thus as an essential value of the common life. There is a reference to the disputes which took place on several occasions between the apostles themselves, who in following Jesus did not cease to be men, children of their time and their people: they were anxious to establish ranks of greatness and authority. Jesus' response was a lesson in humility and willingness to serve (c.f. Matthew 18:3-4; 20:26-28). Then he gave them "his" commandment of mutual love (c.f. John 13:34; 15:12, 17) according to his example. . . .

Certainly, the practice of fraternal love in the common life requires considerable effort and sacrifice. . . . An example of this is found in the first Christian community. They came together immediately after the ascension to pray in unity of heart (c.f. Acts 1:14) and to persevere in fraternal "communion" (2:42), going so far as to share their possessions: "they shared all things in common" (2:44). . . .

The church has always retained a deep memory of—perhaps even a nostalgia for—that early community and, basically, religious communities have always sought to reproduce that ideal of communion in charity as a practical rule of life in common. Their members, gathered by the love of Christ, live together because they intend to abide in this love. Thus they can witness to the church's true countenance, which reflects her soul: charity.

"One heart and one mind" does not mean a rigid, feature-less uniformity, but a deep communion in mutual understanding and reciprocal respect.

It cannot only be a matter, however, of a union of like-mindedness and human affection. The Second Vatican Council, echoing the Acts of the Apostles, speaks of a "sharing of the same spirit" (*Perfectae Caritatis*, 15). It is a question of a unity that has its deepest root in the Holy Spirit, who pours out his love into hearts and spurs different people to help one another on the path of perfection by creating and maintaining an atmosphere of good understanding and cooperation among themselves. As the guarantee of unity in the whole church, the Holy Spirit establishes it and causes it to abide in an even more intense way in communities of consecrated life. . . .[7]

The Apostles Performed "Miracle Signs"

After the resurrection, ascension, and Pentecost, the "miracles signs" performed by Christ are "continued" by the apostles, and later by the saints from generation to generation. The Acts of the Apostles offers us numerous testimonies concerning miracles worked "in the name of Jesus Christ" by Peter (c.f. Acts 3:1-8: 5:15; 9:32-41), Stephen (6:8), and Paul (14:8-10). The lives of the saints, the history of the church and, in particular, the processes for the canonization of the Servants of God, constitute a documentation which, when submitted to the most searching examination of historical criticism and of medical science, confirms the existence of the "power from on high" which operates in the natural order and surpasses it.

It is a question of miraculous "signs" carried out from apostolic times until the present day, and their essential purpose is to indicate that the human person is destined and called to the kingdom of God. These "signs" therefore confirm in different ages and in the most varied circumstances the truth of the gospel, and demonstrate the saving power of Christ who does not cease to call people (through the church) on the path of faith. This saving power of the God-Man is manifested also when the "miracles-signs" are performed through the intercession of individuals, of saints, and of devout people, just as the first sign at Cana of Galilee was worked through the intercession of the Mother of Christ. . . .

Speaking of the miracles which Jesus performed during his earthly ministry, St. Augustine, in an interesting text, interprets them as signs of God's saving power and love and as incentives to raise our minds to the kingdom of heavenly things. "The miracles worked by our Lord Jesus Christ," St. Augustine writes, "are divine works which raise the human mind above visible things to understand what is divine" (*Lectures on the Gospel of John*, 24, 1). Connected with this thought is the reaffirmation of the close link of Jesus' "miracles-signs" with the call to faith. In fact, these miracles demonstrate the existence of the supernatural order, which is the object of faith. Those who observed them and particularly those who experienced them were made aware as if by the touch of a hand that the natural order does not exhaust the whole of reality.

The universe in which we live is not limited merely to the range of things accessible to the senses and even to the intellect itself conditioned by sense knowledge. The miracle is a "sign" that this order is surpassed by the "power from on high," and is therefore also subject to it. This "power from on high" (c.f. Luke 24:49), namely, God himself, is above the entire natural order. It directs this order and at the same time it makes known that—through this order and superior to it—human destiny is the kingdom of God. Christ's miracles are "signs" of this kingdom.[8]

Martyrs Proclaim the Power of Christ's Resurrection

"In the eyes of the foolish they seemed to have died, and their departure was thought to be an affliction, and their going from us to be their destruction." So the author of the Book of Wisdom (3:2-3) proclaimed, long before Christ uttered his words about martyrdom: "But they are at peace" (3:3).

In the act of martyrdom there takes place, therefore, a radical opposition, so to speak, to the criteria and the very foundations of thought.

The human death of the martyrs, a death bound up with suffering and torment—just like the death of Christ on the cross—yields, in a sense, to another superior Reality. The author of the Book of Wisdom writes: "The souls of the righteous are in the hand of God, and no torment will ever touch them" (3:1). This other superior Reality does not wipe out the fact of torment and death, just as it did not wipe out the fact of Christ's Passion and death. It, the invisible "hand" of God, merely transforms this human fact. It already transforms it even in its earthly design, by means of the power of faith that is revealed in the souls of martyrs before torment and suffering: "For though in the sight of men they were punished, their hope is full of immortality" (3:4).

The power of this faith, the power of the hope that comes from God, is stronger than punishment and death itself.

Martyrs bear witness to Christ precisely through this power of faith and hope. They, in fact, similar to him in passion and in death, proclaim simultaneously the power of his resurrection. It is enough to recall here how the first martyr of Christ, the deacon Stephen, died; he departed crying: "Behold, I see the heavens opened, and the Son of Man standing at the right hand of God" (Acts 7:56).[9]

Chapter 9

Witnessing to the Ends of the Earth

*How deep can the roots of the church be, that its branches
have reached the ends of the earth? Its roots are indeed the
crucified and risen Christ. In living out a new chapter in
human history, the apostles proclaimed the Good News to
people of other lands and cultures. God's word was planted in
many lives, bearing sweet and lasting fruit. Through the power
of the Holy Spirit, the apostles embraced the Gentiles. Since
then, people of all races and cultures have discovered their
spiritual roots, which bind all men and women in the fullness
of God's love. As we join the Holy Father in his meditations
on the unbounded witness of the apostles to the risen Christ,
let us pray that nothing will stand in the way of the church's
witness, today and for all time.*

*"Lord, let not the strength of your church rely on numbers
but in its faithfulness and knowledge that you, the crucified
and risen Christ, are the foundation that holds up every living stone. Let the doors of your church always be open to all,
showing no partiality. As we have found your church to be our
true home on earth, let us extend your welcome to all those
who haven't yet found you, and embrace them with the love
that binds your church to you."*

How God's Word Spreads

"The word of God continued to spread, and the number of the disciples increased greatly" (Acts 6:7). So we read, dear brothers and sisters, in the Acts of the Apostles. It is the passionate and moving story of the laborious but relentless fulfillment of the Lord's promise: the progressive spreading of the gospel to all the ends of the earth starting from Jerusalem, the place of Jesus' resurrection and of the first outpouring of the Spirit on the disciples.

It is not the proud report of a human success, but neither is it the satisfying observation of the overwhelming action of a miraculous power. It is rather the amazed contemplation of the efficacy of the saving word which, without special human means, without show or clamor, progressively spreads and conquers. Certainly, human cooperation plays its part: it is the courageous preaching of the first eyewitnesses; it is the effort to clarify and assimilate the demands of the faith; it is the whole community's commitment to make the gospel message accessible to the people of every culture. The Book of Acts, as do the other texts of the New Testament, offers a rich and fascinating account of all this.

The growth of the church, however, is not limited to a simple quantitative expansion. The new members who gradually "join" the community are not some anonymous, shapeless crowd. They are people who are confronted with the proclamation of salvation and make a choice which pledges their lives. The faith penetrates deep into their hearts. It changes them and enlightens them, enabling them to cooperate with mature and responsible freedom in building up the church.

This is affirmed in the first Letter of Peter when it says: "Like living stones, let yourselves be built into a spiritual house" (2:5). There it is, dear brothers and sisters! The church is a "spiritual house, "made up of the "living stones" which are the men and women reborn in Christ. Jesus is the "cornerstone, chosen and precious," the foundation on which the church, under the action of the Spirit, has been building herself throughout the centuries. Almost as if to warn us about the recurring temptations of superficiality and sensationalism, or even of disappointment and weariness, the first Letter of Peter reminds us that the true foundation of the church is deep-seated: it is in the crucified and risen Christ. In him the Christian is called to "sink roots," thus to lend the strength to respond totally to the saving love of God.[1]

Peter Opens the Door to the Gentiles

The premier authority of Peter among the apostles was particularly apparent in resolving the basic problem which the early church had to face: the relationship with the Jewish religion and thus the constitutive basis of the new Israel. It was necessary, that is, to decide to draw the consequences of the fact that the church was neither an offshoot of the Mosaic regime, nor some religious current or sect of ancient Israel.

Concretely, when the problem was posed to the apostles and the first Christian community with the case of the centurion Cornelius requesting baptism, Peter's intervention was decisive. The Acts of the Apostles describes how the event unfolded. In a vision the pagan centurion received from an "angel of the Lord" the order to call on Peter: "Summon one Simon who is called Peter" (Acts 10:5). This order of the angel's includes and confirms the authority possessed by Peter: his decision will be needed for allowing pagans to be baptized. . . .

God shows no partiality. The decisive step was taken immediately after the vision, when the men sent by the centurion Cornelius presented themselves to Peter. Peter could have hesitated to follow them, since Jewish law forbade contact with pagan foreigners, considered to be impure. But the new awareness he had as a result of the vision compelled him to overcome this discriminatory law. In addition, the impulse of the Holy Spirit made him understand that he should accompany these men without delay, for they had been sent to him by the Lord. He abandoned himself completely to fulfilling God's plan for his life. It is easy to suppose that, without the light of the Spirit, Peter would have continued to observe the prescriptions of Jewish law. It was that light, given to him personally so that he would make a decision in conformity with the Lord's views, which guided and supported him in his decision.

And now for the first time, in front of a group of pagans gathered around the centurion Cornelius, Peter gives his testimony about Jesus Christ and his resurrection: "In truth, I see that God shows no partiality. Rather, in every nation whoever fears him and acts uprightly is acceptable to him" (Acts 10:34-35). It is a decision which, because of its relationship to the Jewish mentality regarding the current interpretation of Mosaic law, seemed revolutionary. God's plan, kept hidden from preceding generations, foresaw that the pagans would be "coheirs in the promise of Jesus Christ" (Ephesians 3:5-6), without first having to be incorporated into the religious and ritual structure of the old covenant. This was the newness brought by Jesus, which by his gesture, Peter made his own and applied concretely.

It should be pointed out that the opening begun by Peter bore the seal of the Holy Spirit, who came down upon the group of pagan converts. There is a connection between Peter's word and the action of the Holy Spirit. We read that "While Peter was still speaking these things, the Holy Spirit fell upon all who were listening to the word" (Acts 10:44). A witness to this gift of the Holy Spirit, Peter saw the consequences and said to his "brethren": " 'Can anyone withhold the water for baptizing these people, who have received the Holy Spirit even as we have?' He ordered them to be baptized in the name of Jesus Christ" (10:47).

This formal resolution of Peter's, obviously illumined by the Spirit, took on decisive importance for the church's development by eliminating the obstacles stemming from the observance of the Jewish law. . . .

We know that later the apostle Paul, the Doctor *Gentium*, would be particularly called to proclaim the gospel among the pagans. However, he himself recognized the authority of Peter as a guarantor of the rightness of his own mission of evangelization: having begun to preach the gospel to pagans, he relates, " . . . after three years I went up to Jerusalem to confer with Cephas" (Galatians 1:18). Paul was acquainted with Peter's role in the church and recognized its importance. Fourteen years later he again went to Jerusalem for verification: " . . . so that I might not be running, or have run, in vain" (2:2). This time he spoke not only to Peter but "to those of repute" (2:6). He shows, however, that he regarded Peter as the supreme head. In fact, although in the geo-religious distribution of work Peter was entrusted with the gospel to the circumcised (2:7), he still was the first to preach the gospel to the pagans, as seen in Cornelius's conversion. On that occasion Peter opened the door to all the Gentiles who could be reached at the time.[2]

The Spirit Impels Paul and Barnabas to Witness to the Gentiles

Paul and Barnabas are impelled by the Spirit to go to the Gentiles (c.f. Acts 13:46-48), a development not without certain tensions and problems. How are these converted Gentiles to live their faith in Jesus? Are they bound by the traditions of Judaism and the law of circumcision? At the first Council, which gathers the members of the different churches together with the apostles in Jerusalem, a decision is taken which is acknowledged as coming from the Spirit: It is not necessary for a Gentile to submit to the Jewish law in order to become a Christian (c.f. 15:5-11, 28). From now on the church opens her doors and becomes the house which all may enter, and in which all can feel at home, while keeping their own culture and traditions, provided that these are not contrary to the gospel.

The missionaries continued along this path, taking into account people's hopes and expectations, their anguish and sufferings, as well as their culture, in order to proclaim to them salvation in Christ. The speeches in Lystra and Athens (c.f. Acts 14:15-17; 17:22-31) are acknowledged as models for the evangelization of the Gentiles. In these speeches Paul enters into "dialogue" with the cultural and religious values of different peoples. To the Lycaonians, who practiced a cosmic religion, he speaks of religious experiences related to the cosmos. With the Greeks he discusses philosophy and quotes their own poets (c.f. 17:18, 26-28).

The God whom Paul wishes to reveal is already present in their lives; indeed, this God has created them and mysteriously guides nations and history. But if they are to recognize the true God, they must abandon the false gods which they themselves have made and open themselves to the one whom God has sent to remedy their ignorance and satisfy the longings of their hearts. These are speeches which offer an example of the enculturation of the gospel.

Under the impulse of the Spirit, the Christian faith is decisively opened to the "nations." Witness to Christ spreads to the most important centers of the eastern Mediterranean and then to Rome and the far regions of the West. It is the Spirit who is the source of the drive to press on, not only geographically but also beyond the frontiers of race and religion, for a truly universal mission.[3]

How We Live a Resurrected Life

In the remaining chapters, we consider the practical side of how to live the power of the resurrection. How does the resurrection impact my everyday life here and now? What am I personally called to do to live the resurrection? How can I share more fully in the gift of Christ's death and resurrection? As we join the Holy Father in meditating upon ways we can live and share the resurrected life, let us pray that we never lose sight of the paschal mystery as the central mystery in our new life in Christ.

"Our Lord and our God, we thank you for the resurrected life you have given us. As we live our new life in you, help us to spread the joy of your resurrection. Lead us to always draw strength and power from your sacraments. Let us make a home in our hearts for the Holy Spirit. Let us joyfully share our faith through the gifts you give us. Let us love this world but not be dragged down by it. Let us love each other with your undying love for us. Let nothing separate us from you and from each other. May your love lead all of us home to you."

Chapter 10
Drawing Power from the Blessed Sacrament

When Jesus said, "He who eats my flesh and drinks my blood abides in me, and I in him" (John 6:56), many left him, unable to accept his words. Those who did accept his words in faith remained with him and became his church. By receiving Christ in the Blessed Sacrament, we feed on Jesus' body, blood, soul, and divinity—the food that gives us Christ's own glorified and eternal life. As we join the pope in his meditations on how we can more fully receive Christ in the Eucharist, we pray that our meeting with him in the liturgy will be the source from which we draw grace and new life.

"Our Lord and our God, Word made flesh, on the eve of your death, you gave your church its greatest treasure, your real presence in the Eucharist. You indeed are the heavenly food that sustains our life. Heaven meets earth in our souls when we receive you. Lord, help us always to carry your presence with the deepest reverence, by living our lives according to your will and by generously sharing with others the abundant grace we receive from you in this sacrament."

We Carry Christ within Us

In the sacrament which Jesus institutes during the Last Supper, he gives himself to his disciples: his body and blood in the form of bread and wine. He does what one day he had foretold near Capernaum—and which caused the defection of many. They were so reluctant to accept the words: "I am the living bread, which comes down from heaven; if any one eats of this bread he will live for ever" (John 6:51) . . . And the apostles take, they eat the bread (body), they drink the wine (blood). Jesus says over the chalice: "This is my blood, the blood of the covenant, which is poured out for many" (Mark 14:24).

They receive the body and blood as the food and drink of this Last Supper. And they become participants in the covenant—of the new and eternal covenant which, through this body given on the cross, through this blood poured out during the Passion, is sealed.

Christ adds more: "Truly, I say to you, I shall not drink again of the fruit of the vine until that day when I drink it new in the kingdom of God" (Mark 14:25). This is, therefore, literally the Last Supper. The kingdom of God, the kingdom of future time, is begun in the Eucharist, and it will develop from it until the end of the world.

When the apostles go out after the Last Supper toward the Mount of Olives, all carry in themselves this great mystery which took place in the Cenacle. Christ accompanies them: Christ living on earth. And at the same time they bear Christ within them: Christ-Eucharist.

They are the first of those who later will come to he called *Christo-foroi* (*Theo-foroi*). The participants in the Eucharist were called precisely that. They came out from participating in this sacrament bearing in themselves God incarnate. With him in their hearts they went out among men in their daily lives.[1]

We are thus "*Christo-foroi.*" We carry Christ within us. His body and his blood. His death and resurrection. The victory of life over death. *Christo-foroi*: that is what we are constantly, each day. Today we wish to give this fact a particular public expression. *Christo-foroi*: those who live "through Christ." Just as he lives "through the Father." This is the mystery that we carry within ourselves. The mystery of eternal life in God. Through Christ. "The bread which I shall give for the life of the world is my flesh" (John 6:51).[2]

A Communion between the Risen Christ and the Church

The work of salvation, accomplished by Christ the Lord through his paschal mystery, is not an event belonging exclusively to the past; it is also present in the church's "today," impelling her towards its future fulfillment. This is possible through the power of the Spirit, who acts through the sacred signs of the liturgy, a living and effective memorial of the mystery of redemption. Celebrating the sacred rites, the church, faithful to the command of her Spouse, "opens up to the faithful the riches of the Lord's powers and merits, so that these are in some way made present for all time; the faithful lay hold of them and are filled with saving grace" (*Sacrosanctum Concilium*, 102). . . .

All of this happens, not in an automatic or quasi-miraculous way, but in relation to the faith and the inner disposition of those who participate in it. The liturgy, in fact, presupposes faith and conversion in order to be a lived experience of salvation. . . .

The liturgical celebration is a meeting, dialogue, and communion between the risen Christ and the church, his spouse; he is present and acts in it to give the Spirit. It is the sacred action par excellence (c.f. *Sacrosanctum Concilium*, 7). The church cannot live this communion and be engaged in the mystery of salvation without drawing from this inexhaustible fount. . . .

If we truly desire the liturgical experience to be a fruitful time of communion with God, we must reevaluate the sense of the sacred in the celebration, using to advantage silence, the ability to listen, the intimate joy of contemplating and meeting the Lord, and thereby banishing everything that distracts and that calls attention to the merely human and exterior aspects of the liturgical action.

Finally, we must strive to ensure that the celebration of the divine mysteries be given its central place in the organization of pastoral activity in such a way that all apostolic activity, in a certain sense, will have its beginning and fulfillment therein, precisely because the liturgy is the "summit and foundation" of the church's life and mission.[3]

A Superabundant Source of Spiritual Strength

The life of the risen Christ is distinguished by its power and its richness. He who communicates receives the spiritual power necessary to confront all obstacles and trials, remaining faithful to his commitments as a Christian. Besides, he draws from the sacrament, as from a superabundant source, continuous bursts of energy for the development of all his resources and qualities in a joyful fervor that arouses generosity.

In particular, he draws the life-giving energy of charity. In the church's Tradition, the Eucharist has always been considered and experienced as the sacrament par excellence of unity and love. St. Paul once declared: "Because the loaf of bread is one, we, many though we are, are one body, for we all partake of the one loaf" (1 Corinthians 10:17).

The Eucharistic celebration reunites all Christians, whatever their differences may be, in a unanimous offering and in a meal in which all participate. It gathers them all in the equal dignity of brothers and sisters of Christ and children of the Father. It urges them to respect, to mutual esteem, to mutual service. Communion further gives each one the moral strength necessary to place himself beyond reasons for division and opposition, to forgive injuries received, to give renewed effort in the direction of reconciliation and fraternal accord.

Moreover, is it not particularly significant that the precept of mutual love was formulated by Christ in its greatest expression during the Last Supper, on the occasion of the institution of the Eucharist? May every one of the faithful recall this at the moment of approaching the Eucharistic table and be committed not to belie with his life what he celebrates in mystery.[4]

A Source of Reconciliation with God and Man

Our whole life must be a purifying preparation for our encounter with God: tomorrow in eternity, but also today in the Eucharist. The gospel in today's liturgy reminds us explicitly: "If you are bringing your offering to the altar and there remember that your brother has something against you, leave your offering there before the altar; go and be reconciled with your brother first, and then come back and present your offering" (Matthew 5:23-24). Our participation in the Eucharist, which is a source of our reconciliation with God, must be also a source of our reconciliation with man.

Our everyday life unremittingly sets before us conflicts and tensions, hate and enmity: in our heart, in the family, in the parish community, at work, among nations. The more men yearn for mutual understanding and brotherly harmony, the more unattainable these seem for them. All the more strongly then is the church today aware that God has *entrusted to her the message of reconciliation* (c.f. 2 Corinthians 5:19).

God, who requires of us that we be reconciled with others before we bring our gift to the altar, is at the same time ready to make us disposed to this reconciliation through Christ and his church. For God in Christ "was reconciling the world to himself" (2 Corinthians 5:19) and has given us in the church the precious Sacrament of Reconciliation. True reconciliation between divided and hostile men is possible only when they allow themselves to be reconciled also with God. Authentic brotherly love is founded on love for God, who is the common Father of all.

Let us then be reconciled with all who have something against us, dear brothers and sisters, we who desire to bring our offering to the altar in this sincere love of God and our neighbor. *Let us be reconciled within the community of the church* as brothers and sisters in Christ! Let us have respect toward one another—the scholarly teachers of the faith toward the sentiment and piety of the simple believers; the one who is strongly tied to traditional forms toward those who are concerned, in the spirit of the Second Vatican Council, to bring about an authentic renewal of religious and ecclesiastical life. Instead of bewildering or wounding others, we must rather seek reconciliation and understanding in order that, united in mutual support, in patience and love, we may build up the kingdom of God in our midst, the kingdom of reconciliation and peace. Only in this way will our daily offerings on our altars be graciously accepted by God.[5]

A Thanksgiving from the Heart of the Son

As St. Paul writes: "The Lord Jesus on the night when he was betrayed took bread, and when he had given thanks, he broke it and said: 'This is my body which is for you. Do this in remembrance of me'" (1 Corinthians 11:23-24). Likewise the [synoptic gospels], in their turn, speak of the thanksgiving over the chalice, "Then he took a cup; and when he had given thanks he gave it to them, and they all drank of it. And he said to them, "This is my blood of the covenant, which is poured out for many" (Mark 14:23-24; c.f. Matthew 26:27; Luke 22:17).

The original Greek of the expression "gave thanks" is from *eucaristein*—from which comes Eucharist. Thus then the sacrifice of the body and blood instituted as the Most Blessed Sacrament of the church fulfilled and at the same time superseded those sacrifices of blessing and praise spoken of in the Psalms (*zebah todah*). The Christian communities from the earliest times joined the celebration of the Eucharist to *thanksgiving*, as is shown by a text of the *Didache* (composed between the end of the first century and the beginning of the second, probably in Syria, perhaps even in Antioch):

> *We thank you, our Father, for the holy life of David your servant, which you have made known to us through Jesus Christ your servant. . . .*
> *We thank you, our Father, for the life and knowledge which you have made known to us through Jesus Christ your servant. . . .*

We thank you, our Father, for your holy name,
which you have made to dwell in our hearts, and
for the knowledge, the faith and immortality which
you have made known to us through Jesus Christ
your servant. (Didache 9:2-3; 10:2)

The church's hymn of thanksgiving which accompanies
the Eucharist arises from her inmost heart, and indeed *from*
the very Heart of the Son, who lives to give thanks. It can
rightly be said that her prayer, and indeed her whole earthly
existence, became a revelation of this fundamental truth stated
in the Letter of James: "Every good endowment and every
perfect gift is from above, coming down from the Father of
lights . . ." (James 1:17).

The giving of thanks restores to man the awareness of the
gift bestowed by God "from the beginning," and at the same
time expresses the readiness to reciprocate the gift: to give
with all one's heart to God oneself and everything else. It is,
as it were, a restitution, because everything has in him its
beginning and source.[6]

An Offering of Ourselves as Servants

The Offertory is a privileged moment for all vocations in
the church. All participate in the Offertory, actualizing their
vocations and inserting them into the whole body of Christ,
under the species of bread and wine. . . .

Drawing near to [the] altar with the symbolic gifts of bread
and wine, we profoundly experience this ecclesial mystery of
our vocation. We implore with all our hearts that our vocation
may be fruitful, spiritually fruitful for the church, for others,
for all to whom we are sent and, in the end, for ourselves. First

for others, then for ourselves, because, like Christ, we find ourselves in the condition of "servant." We prepare ourselves to be servants. . . .

We find ourselves in an analogous moment, the preparation of our Eucharist, which is always the Eucharist of Christ, but also our own. Let us awaken this deep awareness in our minds, in our hearts. Let us also arouse this great desire to serve well, to be a good servant, that servant to whom the Lord will also be able to say one day: you have been faithful in daily affairs, faithful in little things, I will give you authority over great things (c.f. Matthew 25:21, 23).

Because, beloved friends, the Eucharist is a tremendous opening to great things, to the greatest thing we can imagine, conceive, or anticipate. The Eucharist is the opening to the mystery of God, the mystery of creation and redemption, the mystery of the Son in the Father and the Father in the Son in the Holy Spirit. Behold, we stand before this mystery. The Eucharist opens this mystery to us.

We must prepare ourselves well, bringing our gifts, the gift of our vocation, to this altar of the Lord. Amen.[7]

A Tide of Charity Flows from the Mass

The teachings of the apostles struck a sympathetic chord from the earliest centuries, and evoked strong echoes in the preaching of the Fathers of the church. St. Ambrose addressed words of fire to the rich who presumed to fulfill their religious obligations by attending church without sharing their goods with the poor, and who perhaps even exploited them: "You who are rich, do you hear what the Lord God says? Yet you come into church not to give to the poor but to take instead." St. John Chrysostom is no less demanding: "Do you wish to honor the body of Christ? Do not ignore him when he is naked. Do not pay him homage in the temple clad in silk only then to neglect him outside where he suffers cold and nakedness. He who said: 'This is my body' is the same one who said: 'You saw me hungry and you gave me no food,' and 'Whatever you did to the least of my brothers you did also to me.' . . . What good is it if the Eucharistic table is overloaded with golden chalices, when he is dying of hunger? Start by satisfying his hunger, and then with what is left you may adorn the altar as well" (*Homilies on the Gospel of Mark*, 50).

These words effectively remind the Christian community of the duty to make the Eucharist the place where fraternity becomes practical solidarity, where the last are the first in the minds and attentions of the brethren, where Christ himself—through the generous gifts from the rich to the very poor—may somehow prolong in time the miracle of the multiplication of the loaves.

The Eucharist is an event and program of true brotherhood. From the Sunday Mass there flows a tide of charity destined to spread into the whole life of the faithful, beginning by inspiring the very way in which they live the rest of Sunday. If Sunday is a day of joy, Christians should declare by their actual behavior that we cannot be happy "on our own." They look around to find people who may need their help. It may be that in their neighborhood or among those they know there are sick people, elderly people, children, or immigrants who precisely on Sundays feel more keenly their isolation, needs, and suffering. It is true that commitment to these people cannot be restricted to occasional Sunday gestures. But presuming a wider sense of commitment, why not make the Lord's Day a more intense time of sharing, encouraging all the inventiveness of which Christian charity is capable? Inviting to a meal people who are alone, visiting the sick, providing food for needy families, spending a few hours in voluntary work and acts of solidarity: these would certainly be ways of bringing into people's lives the love of Christ received at the Eucharistic table.[8]

Why the Eucharist Is the Source and Summit of Christian Life

The Eucharist is the source of the Christian life because whoever shares in it receives the motivation and strength to live as a true Christian. Christ's sacrifice on the cross imparts to the believer the dynamism of his generous love; the Eucharistic banquet nourishes the faithful with the body and blood of the divine Lamb sacrificed for us, and it gives them the strength to "follow in his footsteps" (c.f. 1 Peter 2:21).

The Eucharist is the summit of the whole Christian life because the faithful bring to it all their prayers and good works, their joys and sufferings. These modest offerings are united to the perfect sacrifice of Christ and are thus completely sanctified and lifted up to God in an act of perfect worship which brings the faithful into the divine intimacy (c.f. John 6:56-57). Therefore, as St. Thomas Aquinas writes, the Eucharist is "the culmination of the spiritual life and the goal of all the sacraments" (*Summa Theologica*, III, q. 66).

The angelic Doctor also notes that the "effect of this sacrament is the unity of the mystical body (the church), without which there can be no salvation. Therefore it is necessary to receive the Eucharist, at least by desire (*in voto*), in order to be saved" (III, q. 73). In these words there is an echo of everything Jesus himself said about the necessity of the Eucharist for the Christian life: "Amen, amen, I say to you, unless you eat the flesh of the Son of Man and drink his blood, you do not have life within you. Whoever eats my flesh and drinks my blood has eternal life, and I will raise him on the last day" (John 6:53-54). According to these words of Jesus, the Eucharist is a pledge of the resurrection to come, but it is already a source of eternal life in time. Jesus does not say, "will have eternal life," but "has eternal life." Through the food of the Eucharist, Christ's eternal life penetrates and flows within human life.[9]

Chapter 11

Drawing Power from God's Word

The written word of God has great power to transform our lives. Hearing or reading the Scriptures inclines our hearts and minds to know God ever more intimately and to live according to his commandments. In it we read our own story woven into the great story of God's love for us. As we join the Holy Father in his meditations on how we can draw life from sacred Scripture, let us pray for the grace to receive God's word with open hearts and minds.

"Our Lord and our God, we thank you for your word in Scripture; for your church, which has faithfully preserved and handed down your word to us; and for the light of sacred tradition, which reveals to us the depths of your word. Your word, indeed, is spirit and life. It satisfies our hunger for knowledge that this world cannot give, and ignites our desire to be united with you in eternity. O Lord, we pray that you will open the Scriptures for us. Give us hearts that burn with zeal to know and follow you, and reveal to us all that will help us to glorify you."

Experience Christ's Living Presence through His Word

Christ himself interpreted to the disciples of Emmaus the deeper meaning of what had happened as being connected with the divine plan of salvation as indicated in the words of the holy Scripture: "Beginning then with Moses and all the prophets, he interpreted for them every passage of scripture which referred to him" (Luke 24:27).

At all times God has moved people through the word of his revelation and renewed the church. Let us trust that today, too, the word of God will have sufficient power to awaken new life in the church and to win new followers for Christ. Faith is convincing when it is genuine and is shared with others. Don't be afraid to talk about matters of faith, share your religious experience with one another, seek religious examples to follow. They are to be found right among you. Renew in this manner your lives from the holy Scripture as believed and interpreted in faithfulness to tradition. Read the Scriptures daily, if possible. Meditate on them. Give the word of God a convincing and winning form in your lives. You will experience the living presence of Christ in yourselves through his word.[1]

Receive the Word of God as Spirit and Life

The [first reading], taken from the Book of Nehemiah, reminds us with what veneration the People of God of the Old Testament listened to the words of holy Scripture read by the priest Ezra on the day "consecrated to God": "Ezra opened the book in the presence of all the people. . . . When he had opened the book, all the people rose to their feet. Ezra blessed the great Lord God and all the people answered: Amen, amen!" (Nehemiah 8:5-6).

The Gospel of St. Luke recounts to us the episode when Jesus, at the beginning of his messianic activity in the synagogue of Nazareth, read a verse from the book of the prophet Isaiah which referred precisely to him! May that be an indication to us of how we must read the divine word, with what disposition we must listen to it, and how we must apply it to ourselves.

"Your words, Lord, are spirit and life" (c.f. John 6:63). If we welcome them with a heart disposed in such a way that they become the life of our souls, then what the psalm from today's liturgy expresses with such enthusiasm will take place in us: "The law of the LORD is perfect, refreshing the soul / The decree of the LORD is trustworthy, giving wisdom to the simple / The precepts of the LORD are right, rejoicing the heart / The command of the LORD is clear, enlightening the eye" (Psalm 19:8-9).

May it be so, dear brothers and sisters, in every one of us. May listening to the word of God rejoice our hearts and guide our behavior . . . for the rest of our lives.[2]

Lectio Divina: A Humble and Loving Listening to God's Word

An essential element of spiritual formation is the prayerful and meditated reading of the word of God (*lectio divina*), a humble and loving listening of him who speaks. It is in fact by the light and with the strength of the word of God that one's own vocation can be discovered and understood, loved and followed, and one's own mission carried out. . . .

Familiarity with the word of God will make conversion easy, not only in the sense of detaching us from evil so as to adhere to the good, but also in the sense of nourishing our heart with the thoughts of God, so that the faith (as a response to the word) becomes our new basis for judging and evaluating persons and things, events and problems.

Provided that we approach the word of God and listen to it as it really is, it brings us into contact with God himself, God speaking to us. It brings us into contact with Christ, the Word of God, the Truth, who is at the same time both the way and the life (c.f. John 14:6). It is a matter of reading the "Scriptures" by listening to the "words," "the word" of God, as the Council reminds us: "The sacred Scriptures contain the word of God, and because they are inspired, are truly the word of God" (*Dei Verbum*, 24). The Council also states: "By this revelation, then, the invisible God, from the fullness of his love, addresses people as his friends, and moves among them, in order to invite and receive them into his own company.". . .

A necessary training in prayer in a context of noise and agitation like that of our society is an education in the deep human meaning and religious value of silence as the spiritual atmosphere vital for perceiving God's presence and for allowing oneself to be won over by it (c.f. 1 Kings 19:11-12).[3]

The Fruits of Meditating on God's Word

As the church's spiritual tradition teaches, meditation on God's word, and on the mysteries of Christ in particular, gives rise to fervor in contemplation and the ardor of apostolic activity. Both in contemplative and active religious life, it has always been men and women of prayer, those who truly interpret and put into practice the will of God, who do great works. From familiarity with God's word they draw the light needed for that individual and communal discernment which helps them to seek the ways of the Lord in the signs of the times. In this way they acquire a *kind of supernatural intuition,* which allows them to avoid being conformed to the mentality of this world, but rather to be renewed in their own mind, in order to discern God's will about what is good, perfect, and pleasing to him (c.f. Romans 12:2).[4]

Chapter 12

Drawing Strength from the Holy Spirit

Two millennia ago, the Blessed Mother and the apostles gathered in the Cenacle and devoted themselves to prayer as they waited for the coming of the Holy Spirit. Today, in the same fashion, the church each year prayerfully prepares to receive the Holy Spirit during Pentecost. As the resurrection seals our faith in Christ as Lord and God, Pentecost seals our fate as witnesses of the risen Christ.

In his meditations on the risen Christ's return to the Father and the descent of the Holy Spirit upon us, the pope helps us reflect upon the Third Person of the Trinity as a personal being, how he moves in our lives, and how we can prepare to fully receive him in our hearts. Let us pray that we will come to know more deeply the Paraclete, our counselor and defender.

"O risen Christ, we thank you for sending us the Holy Spirit. Truly he comes, just as you promised. And when he comes, a great wind blows through our souls, washing away the fears and hesitations that keep us from answering your call for us to live and make known your saving power. Through the Holy Spirit, who is one with you and the Father, you are ever present with us and in us.

"O Holy Spirit, we thank you for being the 'sweet guest' of our soul. We pray for the grace to know you ever more *deeply and to be always ready to hear and follow your divine guidance. May we always rely, not on our own strength and understanding, but on the supernatural strength and wisdom you give us. To know and receive you is indeed the enlightenment we had sought and found only in you."*

The Holy Spirit as a Personal Being

In speaking of the Holy Spirit, Jesus frequently uses the personal pronoun "he": "He will bear witness to me" (John 15:26). "He will convince the world of sin" (16:8). "When the Spirit of truth comes, he will guide you into all the truth" (16:13). "He will glorify me" (16:14). From these texts it is evident that the Holy Spirit is a Person, and not merely an impersonal power issuing from Christ (for example, Luke 6:19: "Power came forth from him"). As a Person, he has his own proper activity of a personal character. Jesus, in fact, when speaking of the Holy Spirit, says to the apostles: "You know him, for he dwells in you, and will be in you" (John 14:17). "He will teach you all things, and bring to your remembrance all that I have said to you" (14:26); "He will bear witness to me" (15:26); "He will guide you into all the truth"; "Whatever he hears he will speak" (16:13). He "will glorify" Christ (16:14). The apostle Paul, on his part, states that the Spirit "cries in our hearts" (Galatians 4:6); "he apportions" his gifts "to each one individually as he wills" (1 Corinthians 12:11); "he intercedes for the saints" (Romans 8:27).[1]

The Descent of the Holy Spirit Fully Reveals God as Trinity

The Holy Spirit revealed by Jesus is a personal being (the third Person of the Trinity), with his own personal activity.

However, in the same "farewell discourse," Jesus shows the bonds that unite the Person of the Holy Spirit with the Father and the Son. He announces the descent of the Holy Spirit, and at the same time the definitive revelation of God as a Trinity of Persons.

Jesus tells the apostles: "I will pray the Father, and he will give you another Counselor" (John 14:16); "the Spirit of truth who proceeds from the Father" (15:26), "whom the Father will send in my name" (14:26). The Holy Spirit is therefore a Person distinct from the Father and from the Son and, at the same time, intimately united with them: "He proceeds" from the Father; the Father "sends" him in the name of the Son—and this in consideration of the redemption effected by the Son through his self-offering on the cross. Therefore, Jesus Christ says: "If I go, I will send him to you" (16:7). "The Spirit of truth who proceeds from the Father" is announced by Christ as the Counselor, whom "I shall send to you from the Father" (15:26). . . .

The Holy Spirit reveals the depths of the divinity: the mystery of the Trinity in which the divine Persons subsist, but open to human beings to grant them life and salvation. St. Paul refers to that when he writes in the first Letter to the Corinthians that "the Spirit searches everything, even the depths of God" (2:10).[2]

The Holy Spirit Transforms Us Deep Down

The Holy Spirit is the author of our sanctification: he transforms man deep down, divinizes him, makes him a participant in divine nature (c.f. 2 Peter 1:4), just as fire makes metal incandescent, just as spring water quenches thirst: *fons vivus, ignis, caritas*. Grace is communicated by the Holy Spirit through the sacraments, which accompany man during the whole span of his existence. By means of grace, he becomes the sweet guest of the soul, *dulcis hospes animae*: he dwells in our heart; he is the animator of secret energies, of courageous choices, of unshakable faithfulness. He makes us live in abundance of life: divine life itself.

Precisely through this solicitude about the abundance of life, Christ reveals himself as the Good Shepherd of human souls: the Shepherd who foresees the definitive future of man in God; the Shepherd who knows his sheep (c.f. John 10:14) to the very depths of the inner truth of man, who can speak of himself with the words of St. Augustine: "My heart is restless until it rests in thee."[3]

Ten Days of Prayer to the Holy Spirit

Year after year, the church in her liturgy celebrates the Lord's ascension on the fortieth day after Easter. Year after year, she also spends that period of ten days from ascension to Pentecost in prayer to the Holy Spirit. In a certain sense, the church prepares, year after year, for the anniversary of her birth. She was born on the cross on Good Friday—as the Fathers teach: she revealed this birth of hers to the world on the day of Pentecost, when the apostles were "clothed with power from on high" (Luke 24:49); when they were "baptized with the Holy Spirit" (Acts 1:5)....

"The reinvigorating breath of the Spirit [comes] to awaken slumbering energies in the church, to arouse sleeping charisma, to instill that sense of vitality and joy which at every period of history defines the church herself as young and of topical interest, ready and happy to proclaim again her eternal message to the new times" (Paul VI, *Address to the Cardinals*, December 21, 1973).

This year, too, it is necessary to prepare for acceptance of this Gift. . . . So let us address our prayers to the Holy Spirit in this period. Let us pray for his gifts. Let us pray for the transformation of our souls. Let us pray for fortitude in confessing the faith, for consistency of life with faith. Let us pray for the church, so that she may carry out her mission in the Holy Spirit; so that the counsel and the Spirit of her Bridegroom and his God may accompany her (c.f. S. Bernard, *In Vigilia Nativitatis Domini,* Sermon 3). Let us pray for the union of all Christians: for union in carrying out the same mission.[4]

The Importance of Praying the Novena to the Holy Spirit

In the course of these days, [the church] invites us to take part in the novena to the Holy Spirit. It can be said that, among the various novenas, this is the most ancient one; it takes its origin, in a way, from the institution by Christ the Lord. It is clear that Jesus did not designate the prayers which we are to recite during these days. But certainly, he urged the apostles to spend these days in prayer in expectation of the descent of the Holy Spirit. This urging was valid not only then. It is still valid. And the period of ten days after the Lord's ascension brings with it, every year, the same call of the Master. It also conceals within it the same mystery of grace, connected with the rhythm of liturgical time. It is necessary to take advantage of this time. In it, too, let us try to reflect deeply, in a particular way, and in a certain way to enter the Upper Room together with Mary and with the apostles, preparing our souls to accept the Holy Spirit and his action in us. All this is of great importance for the interior maturity of our faith, of our Christian vocation. And it is also of great importance for the church as a community: May every community in the church, and the whole church as a community of all communities, mature year after year by means of the gift of Pentecost.[5]

The Gift of Strength at the Sacrament of Confirmation

The grace conferred by the Sacrament of Confirmation is more specifically a gift of strength. The Council says that through Confirmation the baptized "are endowed with the special strength of the Holy Spirit" *(Lumen Gentium,* 11). This gift corresponds to the need for greater zeal in facing the "spiritual battle" of faith and charity (c.f. *Summa Theologica,* III, q. 72), in order to resist temptation and give the witness of Christian word and deed to the world with courage, fervor, and perseverance. This zeal is conferred in the sacrament by the Holy Spirit.

Jesus noted the danger of being ashamed to profess the faith: "Whoever is ashamed of me and of my words, the Son of Man will be ashamed of when he comes in his glory and in the glory of the Father and of the holy angels" (Luke 9:26; Mark 8:38). Being ashamed of Christ is often expressed in those forms of "human respect" by which one hides one's own faith and agrees to compromises which are unacceptable for someone who wants to be Christ's true disciple. How many people, even Christians, make compromises today!

Through the Sacrament of Confirmation, the Holy Spirit fills the individual with the courage to profess his faith in Christ. Professing this faith, according to the Council text with which we began, means "to spread the faith by word and deed" as consistent and faithful witnesses.[6]

Confirmation . . . is received only once during life. However, it must leave a lasting mark: precisely because it marks the soul indelibly, it can never be reduced to a distant memory or a fading religious practice, soon exhausted. It is necessary, therefore, to ask ourselves how the sacramental and vital meeting with the Holy Spirit, whom we have received from the hands of the apostles by means of confirmation, can and must last and become more deeply rooted in the lives of each of us. This is shown splendidly in the Pentecost Sequence *Veni Sancte Spiritus*. It reminds us, in the first place, that we must invoke with faith, with insistence, this admirable gift, and it teaches us also how we must invoke it. Come, O Holy Spirit, send us a ray of your light. . . . Perfect Comforter, give us your sweet relief, rest in fatigue, and consolation in suffering. Give us your power, because without it there is nothing in us.[7]

The Holy Spirit Helps Us Discern Truth from Falsehood

If they are docile and faithful to his divine teaching, the Holy Spirit preserves them from error by giving them victory in the continual struggle between the "spirit of truth" and the "spirit of deceit" (c.f. 1 John 4:6). The spirit of deceit which does not acknowledge Christ (c.f. 4:3) is spread by the "false prophets" who are always present in the world, even among the Christian people, with an activity that is sometimes open and even sensational, or sometimes underhanded and sly. Like Satan, they too sometimes masquerade as "angels of light" (c.f. 2 Corinthians 11:14) and present themselves with apparent charisms of prophetic and apocalyptic inspiration. This already occurred in apostolic times. For this reason, St. John warns: "Do not trust every spirit but test the spirits to see whether they belong to God, because many false prophets have gone out into the world" (1 John 4:1).

The Holy Spirit, as Vatican II recalls (c.f. *Lumen Gentium*,

12), protects the Christian from error by enabling him to discern what is genuine from what is false. The Christian will always need good criteria to discern the things he hears or reads in matters of religion, sacred Scripture, manifestations of the supernatural, etc. These criteria are conformity to the gospel, harmony with the teaching of the church established and sent by Christ to preach his truth, the moral conduct of the person speaking or writing, and the fruits of holiness which result from what is presented or proposed.[8]

The Holy Spirit: Our Inner Guide and Teacher

The Holy Spirit teaches the Christian the truth as a principle of life. He shows the concrete application of Jesus' words in each one's life. He enables one to discover the contemporary value of the gospel for all human situations. He adapts the understanding of the truth to every circumstance, so that this truth does not remain merely abstract and speculative, but frees the Christian from the dangers of duplicity and hypocrisy.

To this end, the Holy Spirit enlightens each one personally, to guide him in his conduct, by showing him the way to go and by giving him just a glimpse of the Father's plan for his life. St. Paul seeks this great grace of light for the Colossians: "the spiritual understanding" which can enable them to understand the divine will. In fact, he assures them: "We do not cease praying for you and asking that you may be filled with the knowledge of his [God's] will through all wisdom and spiritual understanding, to live in a manner worthy of the Lord, so as to be fully pleasing, in every good work bearing fruit . . ." (Colossians 1:9-10). For all of us this grace of light is necessary to have a good knowledge of God's will for us and to be able to live our personal vocation fully.[9]

The Holy Spirit Brings Divine Solutions to the Knots of Human Affairs

Problems are never lacking, and they sometimes seem insoluble. But the Holy Spirit helps us in our difficulties and gives us light. He can reveal the divine solution, as he did at the time of the annunciation in regard to the problem of reconciling motherhood with the desire for preserving one's virginity. Even when it is a question of a unique mystery such as the role of Mary in the Incarnation of the Word, the Holy Spirit can be said to possess an infinite creativity to the divine mind, which knows how to loosen the knots of human affairs, even the most complex and inscrutable.

All of this is given and accomplished in the soul by the Holy Spirit through his gifts, the graces which one can carefully discern, not according to the criteria of human wisdom, which is foolishness in God's sight, but with that divine wisdom which can seem foolishness in the eyes of men (c.f. 1 Corinthians 1:18-25). In fact, only the Holy Spirit "scrutinizes everything, even the depths of God" (1 Corinthians 2:10-11). And if there is opposition between the spirit of the world and the Spirit of God, Paul reminds Christians: "We have not received the spirit of the world but the Spirit that is from God, so that we may understand the things freely given us by God" (2:12). Unlike the "natural person," the "spiritual person" (*pneumatikos*) is sincerely open to the Holy Spirit, docile and faithful to his inspirations (c.f. 2:14-16). Thus, he habitually possesses the ability to make right judgments under the guidance of divine wisdom.

A sign that our discernment is in real contact with the Holy Spirit is and will always be adherence to revealed truth as it is proposed by the church's Magisterium. The interior Teacher does not inspire dissent, disobedience, or even merely an unjustified resistance to the pastors and teachers established by him in the church (c.f. Acts 20:28). It belongs to the church's authority, as the Council said in the Constitution *Lumen Gentium* (12), to "not quench the Spirit, but to test everything and retain what is good" (1 Thessalonians 5:12 and 19, 21). This is the direction of ecclesial and pastoral wisdom which also comes from the Holy Spirit.[10]

Chapter 13

Living the Great Commission

What does it really mean for us to live the last words of the risen Christ: "Go therefore and make disciples of all nations, baptizing them in the name of the Father and of the Son and of the Holy Spirit, teaching them to observe all that I have commanded you" (Matthew 28:19-20). Christ gave this commission to the apostles, as well as to Christians of all vocations. To live out this commission is to be rooted in the conviction of the first witnesses of the risen Christ—that he indeed has "all authority in heaven and on earth" to give this command (28:18). In the lives of Christians throughout the ages, this conviction flows out of immeasurable gratitude to Christ, whose faithful witness to the invisible God has made the true God not only known to us, but truly present in our lives. Thus, we too cannot be silent about the saving power that spells the difference between merely existing and truly living. To Christians who have known what it is to live with and without Christ, the conviction to witness to Jesus comes from the realization that he has saved their lives from meaninglessness and spiritual death.

Well aware of the challenges facing all of us in our witness to the risen Christ, the Holy Father meditates upon ways we can share our faith in truth, charity, and love. Let us pray for ongoing conversion, the moving force behind all evangelization, and for faithfulness to Christ's own manner of reaching into the hearts of all he wants to make his own.

"Lord, we pray that the last words you spoke to your apostles before your return to the Father will awaken us to one of our deepest callings in life, to share with others what you have done for us, that we all may find ourselves in you.

"Lord, it is not always easy to live this commission. We sometimes encounter hostilities as we witness to our faith. But, like your apostles, we know we can rely upon the strength that the Holy Spirit gives us to conform our lives to your will. We thank you, Lord, for all those who have made it possible for us to know you, as well as those who strengthen our faith through their life and work. May our gratitude to them move us to share the great gift of faith they have passed on to us. We pray that our faith will grow, first in our own families, and from there yield a great harvest for you."

The Risen Christ's Last Words

"All authority in heaven and on earth has been given to me" (Matthew 28:18). [Today] we celebrate the day that Christ, according to the Gospel of Matthew, pronounced these words. It is the fortieth day after the resurrection, the day on which the new life in Christ reveals its dimension transcending the earth, transcending time: the day of the ascension. On this sacred day there was also revealed the definitive "authority," that is, the authority of the risen Christ. It is "authority in heaven and on earth." Christ possesses this authority, this power, eternally, as Son of the very substance of the Father: God from God; Jesus of Nazareth—as man—won this authority at the price of his cross, Passion, and death. It is the authority which comes from the power of the redemption.

In the name of this authority, Christ issues his last earthly command to his apostles: "Go . . . and make disciples of all nations, baptizing them in the name of the Father and of the Son and of the Holy Spirit, teaching them to observe all that I have commanded you; and lo, I am with you always, to the close of the age" (Matthew 28:19-20). It is the missionary mandate: "The Father has sent me, . . . I send you" (c.f. John 20:21). . . .

Let us return once again to Christ's words on the day of the ascension: "Go . . . and make disciples." [In the second reading] we find a moving echo of this call. It resounds in the letter of the apostle Paul; unleashing itself, so to speak, from the depths of his soul. The apostle writes: "If I preach the gospel, that gives me no ground for boasting. For necessity is laid upon me. Woe to me if I do not preach the gospel" (1 Corinthians 9:16). Why this expression "woe to me"?

Here is the answer: "For if I do this of my own will, I have a reward; but if not of my own will, I am entrusted with a commission" (1 Corinthians 9:17). Therefore, "woe" to him if he did not preach, if he did not carry out the work of the gospel, because the power of Christ's redemption is contained in this mission and this service. Here is contained the price that the Son of God has paid for man: we have been bought at a high price (c.f. 6:20; 7:23).

These penetrating words that burst forth from the depths of the soul of the apostle of the Gentiles tell us how great is the "authority" of the crucified and risen Christ; they tell us what it is in substance. These words never cease to bear witness to the power of the apostolic mandate on the day of the ascension. . . . As is well known, in fact, the man who wrote those words to the Corinthians came to Italy: He gave his life in Rome, together with Peter, for Christ and for the gospel. "What then is my reward?" he asks. "Just this: that in my preaching I may make the gospel free of charge" (1 Corinthians 9:18). Just this: to have made myself "a slave to all" (9:19), indeed, "I have become all things to all men" (9:22) "that I might win the more" (9:19). "I do it all for the sake of the gospel" (9:23).

In the gospel there is a special power for the transformation of man. In it there is a particular power of selfless dedication to others after Christ's example. That which is noblest in man is born of this; that which makes human life fully worthy of man; that for which it is truly worthwhile to live.[1]

Rising to the Call

Dear brothers and sisters, the call to be the witnesses of Christ comes to us from the risen Lord. Before his ascension into heaven, he gave us the firm assurance: "And lo, I am with you always, to the close of the age!" (Matthew 28:20) As the faithful born of the Easter message, we are today sent out into the world in our age by the Lord in our midst in order to give testimony to him and his redeeming truth to our fellow men. . . .

In order to be able to bear witness to Christ and his new life effectively, we must first allow ourselves to be fully possessed by him. But like the disciples on the Sea of Galilee, we are time and again tempted to become weak in faith and give up. Although they had already heard about Jesus' resurrection from Mary Magdalene, although they had actually met him several times, they returned to their boats as if nothing had happened. It sounds like resignation: "I'm going out to fish—we will join you" (John 21:3). The urge to set out for new shores in the footsteps of Jesus Christ appears to have subsided. And even in their own small world as fishermen they had no luck: "All through the night they caught nothing." Although they worked hard all night their nets remained empty. This experience of failure, which easily turns into discouragement, is shared by many people today: in the community, at work, but also in the church. . . .

Often those who have to learn to place their entire hope in resurrection through God have no alternative but to bear their own burden of the cross and burial. It appears that the Lord must take our own means away from us so that our vision is cleared for him. For he seeks our company. As today's gospel says: "Just after daybreak Jesus was standing on the shore." First he needed an honest answer from his disciples, the admission of their own hopelessness and impotence: "Have you caught anything to eat?" They replied: "Not a thing." Then came God's help: "'Cast your net off to the starboard side, and you will find something.' So they made a cast, and took so many fish they could not haul the net in" (John 21:3-6). Suddenly the risen Lord became a reality in their life and changed it. His reality gives a new meaning, and in many cases an unexpected, deeper fulfillment, to everything.[2]

What It Means to Evangelize

The first step of evangelization is to accept the grace of conversion into our own minds and hearts, to let ourselves be reconciled to God. We must first experience God's gracious mercy, the love of Christ which has "reconciled us to himself" and given us "the work of handing on this reconciliation" (2 Corinthians 5:18).[3]

To evangelize does not mean just telling "about Christ." To proclaim Christ means getting the man—the one to whom this proclamation is addressed—to "believe," that is, *to see himself in Christ;* to find again in him the adequate dimension of his own life; simply, to find himself again in Christ.

The one who carries out this work is the man who evangelizes, who proclaims Christ; but above all it is the Holy Spirit, the Spirit of Jesus Christ. The church, which evangelizes, remains the handmaid and instrument of the Spirit.

The fact of finding oneself again in Christ, which is precisely the fruit of evangelization, becomes man's substantial liberation. Service of the gospel is service of freedom in the Spirit. The man who has found himself in Christ has found again the way to the consequent liberation of his own humanity through the overcoming of all his limitations and weaknesses; through liberation from his own situation of sin and from the multiple structures of sin which weigh upon the life of society and of individuals.[4]

The First Form of Evangelization Is Authentic Witness

People today put more trust in witnesses than in teachers, in experience than in teaching, and in life and action than in theories. The witness of a Christian life is the first and irreplaceable form of mission: Christ, whose mission we continue, is the "witness" par excellence (Revelation 1:5; 3:14) and the model of all Christian witness. The Holy Spirit accompanies the church along her way and associates her with the witness he gives to Christ (c.f. John 15:26-27).

The first form of witness is the very life of the missionary, of the Christian family, and of the ecclesial community, which reveal a new way of living. The missionary who, despite all his or her human limitations and defects, lives a simple life, taking Christ as the model, is a sign of God and of transcendent realities. But everyone in the church, striving to imitate the divine Master, can and must bear this kind of witness; in many cases it is the only possible way of being a missionary.

The evangelical witness which the world finds most appealing is that of concern for people, and of charity toward the poor, the weak, and those who suffer. The complete generosity underlying this attitude and these actions stands in marked contrast to human selfishness. It raises precise questions which lead to God and to the gospel. A commitment to peace, justice, human rights, and human promotion is also a witness to the gospel when it is a sign of concern for persons and is directed toward integral human development.

Christians and Christian communities are very much a part of the life of their respective nations and can be a sign of the gospel in their fidelity to their native land, people, and national culture, while always preserving the freedom brought by Christ. Christianity is open to universal brotherhood, for all men and women are sons and daughters of the same Father and brothers and sisters in Christ.

The church is called to bear witness to Christ by taking courageous and prophetic stands in the face of the corruption of political or economic power; by not seeking her own glory and material wealth; by using her resources to serve the poorest of the poor; and by imitating Christ's own simplicity of life. The church and her missionaries must also bear the witness of humility, above all with regard to themselves—a humility which allows them to make a personal and communal examination of conscience in order to correct in their behavior whatever is contrary to the gospel and disfigures the face of Christ.[5]

Every Person Has the Right to Hear the Good News

Nowadays the call to conversion which missionaries address to non-Christians is put into question or passed over in silence. It is seen as an act of "proselytizing"; it is claimed that it is enough to help people to become more human or more faithful to their own religion, that it is enough to build communities capable of working for justice, freedom, peace, and solidarity. What is overlooked is that every person has the right to hear the "good news" of the God who reveals and gives himself in Christ, so that each one can live out in its fullness his or her proper calling. This lofty reality is expressed in the words of Jesus to the Samaritan woman: "If you knew the gift of God," and in the unconscious but ardent desire of the woman: "Sir, give me this water, that I may not thirst" (John 4:10, 15).

The apostles, prompted by the Spirit, invited all to change their lives, to be converted and to be baptized. . . . Conversion to Christ is joined to baptism not only because of the church's practice, but also by the will of Christ himself, who sent the apostles to make disciples of all nations and to baptize them (c.f. Matthew 28:19). Conversion is also joined to baptism because of the intrinsic need to receive the fullness of new life in Christ. As Jesus says to Nicodemus: "Truly, truly, I say to you, unless one is born of water and the Spirit, he cannot enter the kingdom of God" (John 3:5). In baptism, in fact, we are born anew to the life of God's children, united to Jesus Christ and anointed in the Holy Spirit. . . .

All this needs to be said, since not a few people . . . tend to separate conversion to Christ from baptism, regarding baptism as unnecessary. . . . It is also true that many profess an interior commitment to Christ and his message yet do not wish to be committed sacramentally, since, owing to prejudice or because of the failings of Christians, they find it difficult to grasp the true nature of the church as a mystery of faith and love. I wish to encourage such people to be fully open to Christ, and to remind them that, if they feel drawn to Christ, it was he himself who desired that the church should be the "place" where they would in fact find him. At the same time, I invite the Christian faithful, both individually and as communities, to bear authentic witness to Christ through the new life they have received.[6]

Evangelization Begins at Home

To the extent that the Christian family accepts the gospel and matures in faith, it becomes an evangelizing community. Let us listen to Pope Paul VI: "The family, like the church, ought to be a place where the gospel is transmitted and from which the gospel radiates. In a family which is conscious of this mission, all the members evangelize and are evangelized. The parents not only communicate the gospel to their children, but from their children they can themselves receive the same gospel as deeply lived by them. And such a family becomes the evangelizer of many other families, and of the neighborhood of which it forms a part" (*Evangelii Nuntiandi*, 71).

The future of evangelization depends in great part on the church of the home. This apostolic mission of the family is rooted in baptism and receives from the grace of the Sacrament of Marriage new strength to transmit the faith, to sanctify and transform our present society according to God's plan.

Particularly today, the Christian family has a special vocation to witness to the paschal covenant of Christ by constantly radiating the joy of love and the certainty of the hope for which it must give an account: "The Christian family loudly proclaims both the present virtues of the kingdom of God and the hope of a blessed life to come" (*Lumen Gentium*, 35).

The absolute need for family catechesis emerges with particular force in certain situations that the church unfortunately experiences in some places: "In places where anti-religious legislation endeavors even to prevent education in the faith, and in places where widespread unbelief or invasive secularism makes real religious growth practically impossible, 'the church of the home' remains the one place where children and young people can receive an authentic catechesis" (*Catechesi Tradendae*, 68).[7]

The proclamation of the gospel carries with it the constant call to an attitude of conversion on the part of all Christians and must penetrate not only personal and family life but also the social structures, to make them more in conformity with the demands of justice. Let us never forget that only hearts converted and renewed interiorly will improve the moral and human tone of society.

Live, therefore, these demands and infuse into temporal realities the sap of faith in Christ! I am thinking in the concrete of the witness of life and of the evangelizing commitment that the Christian family demands: let spouses live the sacrament of the fruitful and indissoluble union between Christ and the church; let them be the foundation and inspiration of the domestic church, the family, with a commitment to an integral ethical and religious education of the children; let them open to the young the horizons of the various Christian vocations, as a challenge of fullness in contrast to the alternatives of hedonistic consumerism or atheistic materialism.[8]

Dialogue with Our Brothers and Sisters of Other Religions

Inter-religious dialogue is a part of the church's evangelizing mission. Understood as a method and means of mutual knowledge and enrichment . . . [this mission] is addressed to those who do not know Christ and his gospel, and who belong for the most part to other religions. In Christ, God calls all peoples to himself, and he wishes to share with them the fullness of his revelation and love. He does not fail to make himself present in many ways, not only to individuals but also to entire peoples through their spiritual riches, of which their religions are the main and essential expression, even when they contain "gaps, insufficiencies, and errors" (Paul VI, *Opening Address*, Vatican II). All of this has been given ample emphasis by the Council and the subsequent Magisterium, without detracting in any way from the fact that *salvation comes from Christ and that dialogue does not dispense [with] evangelization.* . . .

Dialogue does not originate from tactical concerns or self-interest, but is an activity with its own guiding principles, requirements, and dignity. It is demanded by deep respect for everything that has been brought about in human beings by the Spirit who blows where he wills. Through dialogue, the church seeks to uncover the "seeds of the Word," a "ray of that truth which enlightens all men" (*Nostra Aetate*, 2). These are found in individuals and in the religious traditions of mankind. Dialogue is based on hope and love, and will bear fruit in the Spirit. Other religions constitute a positive challenge for the church: They stimulate her both to discover and acknowledge the signs of Christ's presence and of the working of the Spirit, as well as to examine more deeply her own identity and to bear witness to the fullness of Revelation which she has received for the good of all.[9]

Chapter 14
That We May All Be One

*What does it mean for separated Christians to be one?
What does it really mean for Christians to faithfully respond
to Christ's call to be one family, as God, the Trinity, is a family sharing one life? At the Last Supper, Christ opened his
heart in ardent prayer to the Father, saying: "I do not pray for
these only [the apostles], but also for those who believe in me
through their word, that they may all be one, as you, Father,
are in me and I in you, that they also may be in us" (John
17:20-21). To commonly call Christ "Lord" and yet to be in
a state of disunity is, indeed, a painful reality for Christians
everywhere.*

*As we join the pope in his meditations on the path of
Christian unity, let us pray that we will hear Christ's call
for unity in our hearts and build upon "the recognition of
the primary unity which already exists because of baptism."
This unity, the Holy Father states, "binds the baptized to one
another, . . . a unity that perpetually persists notwithstanding
whatever differences and divisions have arisen."*

|∾ . . . .

*"Our Lord and our God, you alone can conquer all divisions
among your people, as you alone can conquer death. Although
we experience separation, let your love be the love we have for
each other. Purify us from prejudice, pride, and all else that
separates us from you and each other. Help us to keep building*

upon the unity that already exists by working together for peace and justice in the world. We ask you to bless all ecumenical dialogue with the guidance of the Holy Spirit. May the gifts we offer to the cause of Christian unity bring us ever closer to becoming the undivided family you call us to be."

The Soul of the Ecumenical Movement

As Christians today strive to be sources of reconciliation in the world, they feel the need, perhaps more urgently than ever before, to be fully reconciled among themselves. For the sin of disunity among Christians, which has been with us for centuries, weighs heavily upon the church. The seriousness of this sin was clearly shown at the Second Vatican Council, which stated: "Without doubt, this discord openly contradicts the will of Christ, provides a stumbling block to the world, and inflicts damage on the most holy cause of proclaiming the good news to every creature" (*Unitatis Redintegratio*, 1).

Restoration of unity among Christians is one of the main concerns of the church. . . . And this task is for all of us. No one can claim exemption from this responsibility. Indeed, everyone can make some contribution, however small it may seem, and all are called to that interior conversion which is the essential condition for ecumenism. As the Second Vatican Council taught: "This change of heart and holiness of life, along with the public and private prayer for the unity of Christians, should be regarded as the soul of the whole ecumenical movement, and can rightly be called 'spiritual ecumenism'"(*Unitatis Redintegratio*, 8).

The Holy Spirit, who is the source of all unity, provides the body of Christ with a "variety of gifts" (1 Corinthians 12:4), so that it may be built up and strengthened. As the Holy Spirit granted the apostles the gift of tongues, so that all gathered in Jerusalem on that first Pentecost might hear and understand the one gospel of Christ, should we not expect the same Holy Spirit to grant us the gifts we need in order to continue the work of salvation, and to be reunited as one body in Christ? In this we trust and for this we pray, confident in the power which the Spirit gave to the church at Pentecost.[1]

Continue on the Path of Full Unity

Although unity is a gift which we human beings could never achieve on our own, nonetheless we have a duty to seek it and to work for it. It is an essential characteristic of the church, which is always "one, holy, Catholic and apostolic," as we profess in the Creed. But while the church is one, there is disunity among Christians. And the task of restoring unity among all who believe in Christ becomes ever more urgent. The past and present divisions are a scandal to non-Christians, a glaring contradiction of the will of Christ, a serious obstacle to the church's efforts to proclaim the gospel.

The work of ecumenism demands our constant efforts and fervent prayers. It begins with the recognition of that primary unity which already exists because of baptism, a unity which truly binds the baptized to one another and gives them a common share in the life of the Most Holy Trinity. [It is] a unity that perpetually persists notwithstanding whatever differences or divisions have arisen. The words of St. Paul remain forever true: "For as many of you as were baptized into Christ have put on Christ. There is neither Jew nor Greek, there is neither slave nor free, there is neither male nor female; for you are all one in Christ Jesus" (Galatians 3:27-28).

But we must be eager to work for the fullness of unity among the followers of Christ. . . . We rejoice to see the ecumenical progress which has already been achieved: the overcoming of long-standing prejudices, false judgments, and disparaging expressions; the great growth in reciprocal understanding and fraternal respect; the significant progress in dialogue and in collaboration in the service of humanity; and the increasing opportunities for common prayer which respects the different traditions. Let us continue on the path to full unity, looking forward in hope to the day when we shall be truly one, just as the Father and Son are one.

In a certain sense, the unity of Christ's disciples is a condition for fulfilling the mission of the church; not only that, it is a condition for fulfilling the mission of Christ himself in the world. It is a condition for effectively proclaiming and consolidating faith in Christ. Thus Jesus prayed: "That they may all be one . . . so that the world may believe that you have sent me . . . that they may become perfectly one so that the world may know that you have sent me and have loved them even as you have loved me" (John 17:21, 23). . . .

See every person as a child of God. The gift of unity which the church has received from God gives her a special responsibility in the human family: namely, to promote dialogue and understanding among all, to work for unity and peace in our divided world.

Conflicts and tensions abound today. Nations are divided between East and West, North and South, friend and enemy. And within the borders of every country . . . can be found opposing groups and factions, rivalries arising from prejudice and ideologies, from historical stereotypes and ethnic barriers, and from a variety of other factors, none of which are worthy of our human dignity.

It is in this divided world that the church is sent forth today to promote harmony and peace. In charity and truth she goes forth: in that charity which sees every person as a child of God, as a brother or sister of equal dignity—regardless of his or her social status, regardless of his or her race or religion.[2]

Chapter 15

Be In the World but Not Of the World

*How do we live our lives in the world without being con-
sumed by the world? How do we reconcile the demands of
earthly life with our ultimate and eternal destiny? On the eve
of his passion, Christ prayed to the Father, "They are not of
the world, even as I am not of the world. Sanctify them in the
truth.... And I consecrate myself, that they also may be consecrated in truth" (John 17:16-17, 19). The living God, the pope
reminds us, meets us in Jesus Christ, "and nothing and no one
should separate you from this love of God in Christ."[1]*

*As we join the Holy Father in his meditations on how to
live a life "in the world but not of the world," let us pray that
we will live in such a way that we can meet the risen Lord—in
prayer as well as in our daily affairs.*

*"Lord, through your death and resurrection, our life in the
world and our life beyond it have become happily reconciled.
You asked the Father to consecrate us in the truth that sets us
free—free to live our lives in the joy of knowing who we are,
where we come from, and where we are going. And so it has
become our joy to be pilgrims on this earth, even as we know
that this is not our real home. Help us always to make our every
step in this earthly pilgrimage a path to our heavenly home.
Let not the attractions of this world lead us astray from you,
our true and everlasting light. As you consecrate yourself for*

us, we pray for the grace to consecrate our lives and the lives of our families to you."

Always Look for the Light in the Darkness of Our World

You are the guardians of the flame of hope in this world. Just as the fire which you kindled on Pentecost lights up the night . . . so you too should always look for the light in the darkness of your lives and your world. . . .

You do not want your lives to be meaningless and of no importance, but that they be successful and happy. . . . To the all-decisive question of how to obtain this, there can be only one answer for me and I hope for you too: Faith! For "faith" means exactly this: to count on the living God down to your very life fibers, and to live your daily life through him, with him, and in him.

God himself is indeed extraordinary; he transcends the powers of our imagination. In our epoch, we have been permitted to have some insights into the secrets of life, thanks to the natural sciences, insights into the grandiose laws of order of the macrocosm and microcosm, behind which we are able to see the power of God the Creator. And this God is extraordinary, for he himself became one of us, he entered into the venture of life with us. Together with this God who transcends all human limits, your lives too can become an extraordinarily rich and fascinating adventure.

This living God meets you in Jesus Christ. In him, in Jesus Christ, the entire being of God is manifested. It is love pure and simple. With this love, God addresses each and every one of you as a son or daughter. And nothing and no one should separate you from this love of God in Christ (c.f. Romans

8:39) in which your whole life with all its mysteries is safe and secure.

Each individual meets Christ and his peace-giving message in a very personal way. I encourage you: Go to him. Let yourselves be spoken to by him. Talk with him. He will teach you the basic principles of action by which life is to be mastered in a manner worthy of the human being. He will free you from manipulation and being taken in by fashion trends and opinion makers. He will lead you to the path by which you will recognize yourselves and be able to find out who you are, why you are living, and what is the goal of your life. He will lead you to your eternal destiny in God.[2]

Culture a Listening Heart

"My sheep hear my voice. I know them, and they follow me" (John 10:27). Meditating on these words, we understand that no one can claim to be a follower of Christ unless he or she listens to his voice. This is not to be understood simply as hearing, but as attentive listening, such as to make possible a profound mutual recognition which gives rise to a generous, committed following expressed in the words "and they follow me." We can summarize by saying that it means listening not with the ears alone, but with the heart. . . .

The metaphor of the shepherd and sheep thus reveals the very close personal relationship which Jesus wants to establish with us. He is the guide, master, teacher, and model; he is especially our Redeemer. . . . However, he is also the friend, brother, and bridegroom, the faithful and jealous guardian of each of us; this concerns the affective relationship between him and us, a relationship so intimate and deep that it has no equal. There is no true listening without the heart, a listening heart. A listening heart alone can create such a relationship between us and Jesus, our Good Shepherd.[3]

Prayer Should Be Put before Everything Else

In prayer we seek, find, and converse with God, just as we would with an intimate friend (c.f. John 15:15). We can speak of our sorrows and joys, our weaknesses and problems, and our desires to be better and to help others to be better too.

The gospel reminds us of "the need to pray continually and not lose heart" (Luke 18:1). Therefore, every day dedicate some time to conversing with God. This is a sincere proof of your love for him, for love always seeks to be near the beloved. This is why prayer should be put before everything else. Whoever does not understand this, or does not put it into practice, cannot excuse himself by saying he has no time; he has no love.[4]

Human History Must Be Seen in the Perspective of Eternity

"Do not labor for the food which perishes, but for the food which endures to eternal life, which the Son of man will give to you" (John 6:27).

God became incarnate to illuminate, nay more, to be the meaning of man's life. This must be believed with deep and joyful conviction; it must be lived with constancy and consistency; it must be proclaimed and testified, in spite of the tribulations of the times and hostile ideologies, nearly always so insinuating and overwhelming.

And in what way is Jesus the meaning of man's existence? He himself explains it with consoling clarity: "My Father gives you the true bread from heaven. For the bread of God is that which comes down from heaven, and gives life to the world. . . . I am the bread of life, he who comes to me shall not hunger, and he who believes in me shall never thirst" (John 6:32-33, 35). . . .

It is clear that Jesus does not eliminate normal concern and pursuit of daily bread and of everything that can make human life more advanced, more highly civilized, more satisfying. But life passes inevitably. Jesus points out that the real meaning of our earthly existence lies in eternity, and that the whole of human history with its dramas and its joys must be seen in the perspective of eternity.[5]

How to Rise Above Temptation

"I give them eternal life and they shall never perish. No one shall snatch them out of my hand" (John 10:28). . . . Eternal life belongs to the future. Our future in Christ is eternal life. Whoever is "his," Christ's, that is, whoever accepts the gift of grace and does not reject it through sin will not be lost; indeed, no one can steal them from his hand nor the hand of his Father, who is greater than all. . . . It is the "evil one" (c.f. 17:15), the great enemy of God and of his beloved creatures, who seeks to snatch eternal life from us. However, the evil one is not able to do anything against God and against us if we do not first open our souls to him in response to his deceptive allurements. Therefore every time we approach the Lord we must renew our baptismal promises whereby we renounce Satan in order to give ourselves over to faith in Christ the Lord. This is the path of Christian life, the path of Easter joy. Christians are sure of this, and they show that, like the apostles and the first-generation believers, they are living according to Jesus and not according to the world. . . . Sometimes this fidelity demands sacrifice and persecution, not only in the early days, but in our era, too, in our century, as we know quite well; however, as we heard in the passage from the Book of Revelation, the multitude of the saved achieved happiness precisely by passing through the great period of trial and made their robes white in the blood of the Lamb, the Redeemer.[6]

Chapter 16
"Love One Another as I Have Loved You"

How can we truly love each other as Christ has loved us (John 15:12)? Jesus, who is Love himself, made known to us the love that knows no bounds. It is the love that makes others first, ourselves last; the love that conquers all strife; the love that says, "Father, let thy will, not mine, be done" (c.f. Matthew 26:39). Through Christ's resurrection, we have come to know the fullness of God's love for us, the love that knows no death. Jesus himself became the measure of all love, the love we are all called to live.

In his meditations on Jesus' new commandment to "love one another" (John 13:34), the Holy Father reflects upon the "heart of the kingdom of God in mankind and in history," the heart and synthesis of Jesus' teaching.[1] As we meditate on this heart of the kingdom and the heart of our very existence, let us pray that we will always love each other with God's own love for us.

"Our Lord and our God, through your resurrection, the love with which you laid down your life on the cross became the love that rolls away the heavy stone that entombs our hardened hearts. Help us to love each other with your undying love. Let us enter fully into your love for us, as you entered our humanity to lead us by the hand on the path of eternal love. Help us to die to our selfish ways, as you put selfishness to death on the cross. May our lives be a perfect offering of love to you and to one another."

God's Love in the Human Heart

Love enables people to dwell spiritually in one another. This is true at the human level, and it happens in an even deeper way at the divine-human level. "If a man loves me . . . my Father will love him, and we will come to him and make our home with him" (John 14:23). *Love for Christ thus draws the Father's love* and enables the Son and the Father to be present in the human heart, to give themselves intimately to man. This "gift" is the work of the Holy Spirit, who is uncreated love. Poured out into the human heart, he brings it about that the whole Blessed Trinity is present in man and dwells in him.

This indwelling, which springs from love and enriches love, demands to be expressed in truth. Whoever loves Jesus keeps his word, that word of which he says: "The word which you hear is not mine but the Father's who sent me" (John 14:24). Whoever loves Jesus lives by his gospel.[2]

Christ as Lord and Servant of Our Inmost Self

"I am the good shepherd," Jesus says. "I know my own and my own know me, as the Father knows me and I know the Father" (John 10:14-15). How marvelous this knowledge is! What knowledge! It reaches as far as eternal Truth and Love, the name of which is the "Father"! That particular knowledge, which gives rise to sheer trust, comes precisely from this source. Mutual knowledge: "I know and they know."

This is not abstract knowledge, a purely intellectual certainty, which is expressed in the sentence, "I know everything about you." Such knowledge, in fact, arouses fear; it induces one, rather, to withdraw within oneself: "Do not touch my secrets, leave me alone." . . . Christ says, on the contrary: "I know my own," and he says it of the liberating knowledge which brings forth trust. For, although man defends access to his secrets; although he wants to keep them for himself, he has a still greater need, "he is hungry and thirsty" for Someone before whom he could open up, to whom he could manifest and reveal himself.

Man is a person; the need of secrecy and the need of revealing himself belong at the same time to the "nature" of the person. Both these needs are closely united. One is explained by means of the other. Both together indicate, on the contrary, the need of someone before whom man could reveal himself. Certainly, but even more he needs Someone who could help man to enter his own mystery. That "Someone" must, however, win absolute trust; he must, revealing himself, confirm that he is worthy of this trust. He must confirm and reveal that he is the Lord and, at the same time, the Servant of man's interior mystery.

Christ revealed himself precisely in this way. His words: "I know my own and my own know me" find a definitive confirmation in the words that follow: "I lay down my life for the sheep" (c.f. John 10:11-15). That is the interior profile of the Good Shepherd.[3]

Love Is the Law of Abiding in Christ

"Abide . . . " The word that returns most often during the readings of the Fifth Sunday of Easter [John 15:4-5] is precisely the word "abide." With this word the risen Christ, who had first been crucified, invites us to union with him. . . .

In what does this "abiding" in Jesus Christ consist? St. John himself, who included the allegory of the vine in his gospel, offers an answer to this question as author of the first letter. "All who keep his commandments abide in him (God), and he (God) in them" (1 John 3:24). This is the most evident proof.

The apostle almost seems to hesitate in answering the question whether it is possible to establish and ascertain, with the help of some criterion that is verifiable, such a mysterious reality as the abiding of God in man, and thanks to that of man in God. This reality is strictly spiritual in nature. Is it possible to ascertain, to check this reality? Can man have the certainty that his works are good, pleasing to God, and that they serve his abiding in his soul? Can man be certain that he is in a state of grace?

The apostle answers this question as if he were answering himself and us at the same time: "If our hearts do not condemn us, we have confidence before God" (1 John 3:21), the confidence that we abide in him and he in us. And if, on the contrary, we have reasons for apprehension, it is from active love of God and of our brothers that we will be able to derive interior certainty and peace; we will be able to "reassure our hearts before him whenever our hearts condemn us for God is greater than our hearts, and he knows everything" (c.f. 3:19-20). Then, too, we do not cease to be in the range of his love, which can change the state of sin into the state of grace and make our heart once more the dwelling of the living God. All that is necessary is our response to his love. *Love is the principle of divine life in our souls.* Love is the law of our abiding in Christ: of the branch in the vine.

Let us love, therefore, St. John writes, let us love "in deed and in truth" (1 John 3:18). Let our love prove its interior truth by means of deeds. Let us defend ourselves from the appearances of love. . . . "Let us not love in word or speech but in deed and in truth. By this we shall know that we are of the truth, and reassure our hearts before him" (3:18-19). "And by this we know that he abides in us, by the Spirit which he has given us" (1 John 3:24).[4]

God's Love Is Fully Revealed in Christ

"This is my commandment: love one another as I have loved you" (c.f. John 15:12). Dear brothers and sisters, during the joyful period of Eastertide, we [celebrate] the fullness of God's love for mankind revealed and communicated to us through his Son who died and rose. [Today's liturgy] leads us to reflect on this great "gift" from which comes the commandment to love one another.

Let us, first of all, think about God's love for mankind which is fully revealed in Christ, his Son. "God is love," as the apostle John reminds us. He is love because he is "the communion" which unites the Father, Son, and Holy Spirit in the Trinity. He is love because he is a "gift." God's love, in fact, is not closed within itself, but expands and flows into the hearts of everyone he has created, calling them to be his children.

God's love is love which is freely given; it fulfills man's expectations and needs. "It is not we who loved God, but he who loved us" (c.f. 1 John 4:10). He loved us first. He took the initiative. This is the great truth which illuminates and explains everything that God has done and continues to do in the history of salvation.

God's love embraces everyone. Furthermore, God's love is not limited to just a few people but is addressed to all men. It embraces and includes everyone, inviting them to form one family. The apostle Peter confirms this when he speaks about evangelization to the many people gathered together in the house of Cornelius the centurion: "God," he affirmed, "does not have favorites, but anybody of any nationality who fears God and does what is right is acceptable to him" (c.f. Acts 10:34-35).

There are no limits to God's love for mankind: it does not recognize barriers of race or culture; it is universal; it is for everyone. It only asks us to be open to it and to welcome it; it only asks for honest and willing human soil to fertilize.

God's love is concrete. Finally, it is a concrete love, made up of words and gestures, which touches man in different situations, even in suffering and oppression, because it is love which frees and saves, which offers friendship and creates communion. All of this comes from the gift of the Spirit poured out as a gift of love into the hearts of believers to enable them to glorify God and announce his wonders to all peoples.

The contemplation of God's love demands a response and commitment. But which ones? we must ask ourselves. God's word, which we have just heard, fulfills our expectations.

First of all, man is asked to let himself be loved by God. This happens when one believes in his love and takes it seriously, when one accepts the gift of love into one's own life so that one is transformed and formed by it, especially in the relationships of solidarity and brotherhood which unite people.

Jesus Christ asks those who have been touched by the Father's love to love one another and to love everyone as he loved them. The originality and novelty of his commandment lies in the word "as," which means freely given, universal openness, concreteness of words and actions, a capacity to give even to the supreme sacrifice of oneself. In this way, his love can spread itself, transform the human heart, and make of all a community gathered in his love.

Jesus again asks his people to abide in his love, that is, to live firmly in communion with him, in a constant relationship of friendship and dialogue. This is in order to experience full joy, to find the strength to observe the commandments and, finally, to bear the fruit of justice, peace, holiness, and service.[5]

Epilogue

A Personal Testimony

by Jo Garcia-Cobb

"I will tell what he did for my soul." (Psalm 66:16)

This book is the fruit of a life-changing Easter experience that occurred in 2003. Eight years before, Keith had converted to Catholicism, and I had returned to the practice of my Catholic faith. We would like to share some aspects of this journey—with a focus on my experience—to provide a context for the prayers we have written in the introductions to the Holy Father's meditations. This sharing is also a response to the call of Pope John Paul II to more deeply reflect upon our own personal salvation history and to share our story with others.

Sometimes it takes great darkness to see great light. Lent of 2003 was, for me, a time of deep darkness, the end of which I could not see at the time. Not only could I not forgive a dear friend who had done his family a great wrong, but I also was beset with a gnawing lack of certainty about the cornerstone of my convictions as a Christian, the belief that Jesus Christ is God. As a cradle Catholic who left the church for several years and explored various religions and spiritual traditions, I returned in 1995 with a baggage of conflicting ideas about the identity of Jesus Christ.

Whenever I recited the Creed during Mass, I felt a disturbing lack of integrity on my part, not because I did not believe that Jesus Christ was God, but because I was not absolutely certain that he was God. I had read and heard Scripture for many years as a Catholic, and had known the transforming power of the sacraments in my life, but the doubting Thomas in me could not arrive at a point of certainty about my most deeply held conviction. During the Lenten season of 2003, this uncertainty came to a head. To participate in the sacrifice of the Mass, recite the Creed, receive the Eucharist, and be part of the body of Christ while being uncertain about the lordship of Jesus Christ was like living with a spouse I did not know, and therefore could not trust with my life. I sincerely believed, but my intellect could not cease questioning my belief. I was getting very weary of my questioning, and simply wanted to rest in Truth.

The great philosopher Blaise Pascal once proposed a wager, recorded in his *Pensées*, which applies to pursuing the certainty about the true identity of Jesus Christ: "You must wager. It is not optional. You are embarked. Which will you choose then? . . . You must of necessity choose. . . . Let us weigh in the gain and the loss in wagering that God is. Let us estimate these two chances. If you gain, you gain all; if you lose, you lose nothing. Wager, then, without hesitation that he is. In other words, if you wager that God is, and live accordingly, you cannot lose either way. If God is, you win all, and if God is not, you lose nothing. The opposite is also true: If you wager that God is not, and in fact God is, you lose everything and gain nothing."

I had come to a point when I knew I had everything to lose if I did not cross the chasm between uncertainty and faith, but I was not sure what the bridge was between them. One day, I visited our church in Ashland, Oregon, when there was no one else there, and prayed before the Eucharist: "Jesus, if you are really here, please tell me who you really are. People say different things about you. Some say you're God. Others say you're not. And please, help me get over the nightmare of our friend's unfaithfulness. Help me to forgive. I've tried very hard, but I can't seem to do it. Please also help me to overcome the personal weaknesses I have been trying to overcome for years. You know what they are, Lord."

Our family did our best to go to daily Mass and to make a good confession during Lent. When Easter Sunday came around, it was glorious, as every great feast in the church is made glorious by what is celebrated and how it's celebrated. But my heart was still heavy with hurt and unforgiveness, and the question I had posed to God was still awaiting an answer. On Easter Wednesday, however, something curious happened. It was the day when the gospel reading during Mass was about the two disciples on their way to Emmaus (Luke 24:13-35). As I listened to this reading, I noticed that I was hearing Scripture as I had never heard it before. It was speaking straight to my heart. My heart, to paraphrase the disciples' words from this same reading, "burned within me." I started crying, and I could not stop crying until the end of the Mass.

For the rest of Easter, we continued to go to daily Mass, and every single day at Mass I could not keep the tears from pouring out. They were, all at once, tears of repentance, tears of joy, and tears from being overcome with a love so great it was difficult to contain it. Things I had done that hurt others, even those from long ago, resurfaced in my memory during parts of the Mass that allowed for quiet prayer, especially during Communion. The joys and the sorrows of people I knew, whether they were close friends or not, flooded my heart and, somehow, became my own. I was no longer an island, I was home! "My Lord and my God, thank you," I prayed over and over again. Above all, I could no longer approach the Eucharist with the same casualness that I did before. My spirit shook in awe and reverence during the consecration and Communion. Each day, I would come away from Mass feeling that I had been bathed in my own tears. The hardness in my heart was melting away.

By the time the Easter season came to an end on the feast of Pentecost, I began to feel like a new person. The anger and the pain in my heart had given way to a surrender and trust that God's saving power was at work in our friend's life. My uncertainty about Jesus Christ as God had been transformed into an inner certainty that put to rest my restless questioning and continues to bear sweet fruit in our lives.

Although I was very much aware of God's work in my soul during Easter of 2003, I was not completely clear about why this happened at just this time in my life. I wondered why this experience didn't happen before; why I had not recognized the risen Christ in Scripture and in the Eucharist until later in life. Life, I thought, would have been *very* different had this happened earlier. I also wondered what other people went through during Easter and how Christians have encountered the risen Christ over the centuries.

Shortly after I started to think a lot about these questions, my husband and I received a call from an editor, who asked if we were interested in putting together a book of Pope John Paul II's Easter meditations. I asked her to give us a week to pray and think about it. During that week, I went over the pope's writings on the resurrection and began to see the incredible richness and depth of the church's Easter experience. I also became aware of the fact that Easter was not meant to be a passing season of the year, but has always been regarded in the church as a season of profound and lasting transformation. In reading the early church fathers' writings on the meaning and history of the liturgical celebration of Easter (Cantalamessa, *The Mystery of Easter; Easter in the Early Church*), I began to see why Easter was everything in the life of the early church, and can mean everything in the life of today's church.

My husband and I, of course, proceeded to work on this book, which not only answered questions that arose from our Easter experience, but has prolonged our Easter into a lifelong adventure of living out the joy, as well as the challenge, of Christ's resurrection.

Citations

Live in the Joy of the Resurrection
1 Homily, April 21, 1979.
2 Angelus, November 30, 1986.
3 General Audience, April 22, 1992.

Introduction
1 General Audience, March 1, 1989.
2 General Audience, April 14, 1993.
3 General Audience, April 14, 1982.

Part I: Knowing the Resurrection
1. The Resurrection as the Person of Jesus Christ
1 *Urbi et Orbi*, April 19, 1992.
2 Homily, June 6, 1991.
3 Address, To the Youth of the World (5), March 31, 1985.

2. The Resurrection as History
1 Homily, February 23, 2000.
2 Homily, March 30, 2002.
3 Homily, April 21, 1984.
4 Homily, March 29, 1986.
5 Homily, March 25, 1989.
6 Encyclical, *Mulieris Dignitatem* (3), August 15, 1988.
7 Angelus, March 22, 1987.

3. The Resurrection as Mystery
1 *Urbi et Orbi*, April 11, 1982.
2 General Audience, March 1, 1989.
3 General Audience, April 22, 1992.
4 General Audience, April 6, 1988.
5 General Audience, June 8, 1983.
6 Homily, May 18, 1980.

Introduction: The Resurrection as a Passage
1 General Audience, March 22, 1989.
2 General Audience, March 15, 1989.

4. **From Unbelief to Faith**
   [1] Homily, April 2, 1989.
   [2] General Audience, October 28, 1987.
   [3] Homily, June 29, 1979.
   [4] Homily, January 25, 1996.
   [5] Homily, January 25, 1985.
   [6] Homily, February 1, 1986.
   [7] Homily, May 20, 1984.
   [8] Homily, February 1, 1986.
   [9] General Audience, October 21, 1987.
   [10] Homily, May 3, 1987.
   [11] General Audience, February 22, 1989.
   [12] Homily, April 22, 1990.

5. **From Sin to Holiness**
   [1] Angelus, January 24, 1993.
   [2] Homily, February 17, 1988.
   [3] General Audience, November 15, 1989.
   [4] Meditation, August 23, 1997.
   [5] *Ibid.*
   [6] General Audience, April 15, 1992.
   [7] Homily, May 30, 1982.

6. **From Death to Immortality**
   [1] Homily, April 15, 1995.
   [2] Homily, April 23, 1995.
   [3] Encyclical, *Evangelium Vitae* (37-38), March 25, 1995.
   [4] General Audience, May 27, 1992.
   [5] General Audience, March 15, 1989.
   [6] Homily, April 27, 1986.
   [7] Homily, August 15, 1993.
   [8] Homily, August 15, 1995.

Part II: Living the Resurrection

7. **Preparing for the Coming of the Holy Spirit**
   [1] Homily, April 29, 1989.
   [2] Homily, May 21, 1995.
   [3] Homily, April 29, 1989.

[4] *Regina Caeli*, May 4, 1986.
[5] General Audience, January 29, 1992.

8. **How the Holy Spirit Moved through the Apostles**
   [1] Homily, May 18, 1997.
   [2] Homily, April 29, 1995.
   [3] Encyclical, *Redemptoris Missio* (24), December 7, 1990.
   [4] General Audience, October 2, 1991.
   [5] General Audience, March 13, 1991.
   [6] Homily, June 29, 1986.
   [7] General Audience, December 14, 1994.
   [8] General Audience, January 13, 1988.
   [9] Homily, October 5, 1980.

9. **Witnessing to the Ends of the Earth**
   [1] Homily, May 8, 1993.
   [2] General Audience, January 13, 1993.
   [3] Encyclical, *Redemptoris Missio* (24-25), December 7, 1990.

10. **Drawing Power from the Blessed Sacrament**
    [1] Homily, June 10, 1982.
    [2] Homily, June 18, 1987.
    [3] Homily, January 14, 1990.
    [4] General Audience, June 8, 1983.
    [5] Homily, June 15, 1984.
    [6] General Audience, July 29, 1987.
    [7] Address, October 22, 1987.
    [8] Apostolic Letter, *Dies Domini* (71-72), July 5, 1998.
    [9] Homily, April 8, 1992.

11. **Drawing Power from God's Word**
    [1] Homily, May 3, 1987.
    [2] Homily, January 23, 1983.
    [3] Apostolic Exhortation, *Pastores Dabo Vobis* (47), March 25, 1992.
    [4] Apostolic Exhortation, *Vita Consecrata* (94), March 25, 1996.

12. **Drawing Strength from the Holy Spirit**
    [1] General Audience, April 26, 1989.
    [2] General Audience, April 26, 1989.

[3] Angelus, May 10, 1981.

[4] General Audience, May 30, 1979.

[5] General Audience, May 30, 1979.

[6] General Audience, April 1, 1992.

[7] Homily, June 25, 1980.

[8] General Audience, April 24, 1991.

[9] *Ibid.*

[10] *Ibid.*

13. Living the Great Commission

[1] Homily, May 8, 1986.

[2] Homily, May 2, 1987.

[3] Homily, September 15, 1988.

[4] General Audience, February 14, 1979.

[5] Encyclical, *Redemptoris Missio* (42-43), December 7, 1990.

[6] *Ibid*, (46-47).

[7] Apostolic Exhortation, *Familiaris Consortio* (51-52), November 22, 1981.

[8] Homily, February 4, 1985.

[9] Encyclical, *Redemptoris Missio* (55-56), December 7, 1990.

14. That We May All Be One

[1] Homily, May 30, 1982.

[2] Homily, February 6, 1986.

15. Be In the World but Not Of the World

[1] Homily, June 15, 1984.

[2] *Ibid.*

[3] Homily, May 10, 1992.

[4] Homily, April 7, 1987.

[5] Homily, August 5, 1979.

[6] Homily, May 10, 1992.

16. Love One Another as I Have Loved You

[1] General Audience, April 27, 1988.

[2] Homily, May 21, 1995.

[3] General Audience, May 16, 1979.

[4] Homily, May 13, 1979.

[5] Homily, May 5, 1991.

Glossary

Angelus: a short practice of devotion in honor of the incarnation, repeated three times each day: morning, noon, and evening. Pope John Paul II often used the occasion, after praying the Angelus, to make a short address to those in the audience.

charism: a gift of some specific ability or capacity that is used for building the body of Christ.

Christo-foroi: Greek, meaning all who carry Christ within themselves.

communio ecclesialis: Latin, meaning church community; usually refers to the small community that included the apostles, Jesus' mother, and Christ's close disciples, who gathered following the ascension to pray together in preparation to receive the Holy Spirit.

covenant: an agreement between two persons that is obligatory on both parties; in a religious context, it refers to the permanent, binding agreement between God and his chosen people.

Dei Verbum: Latin, meaning "God's Word," a Vatican II document with the English title, "The Dogmatic Constitution on Divine Revelation," promulgated on November 18, 1965.

Didache: a systematic teaching; similar to *didactic.* The Didache referred to here is the Lord's teaching through the twelve apostles—a short treatise, most likely written in the first century—which was accounted by some of the early church fathers as next in importance to Scripture. It was intended for the instruction of new converts.

Dies Domini: Latin, meaning "Day of the Lord," an apostolic letter with the subtitle, "On Keeping the Lord's Day Holy," promulgated by Pope John Paul II on July 5, 1998.

Dominum et Vivificantem: Latin, meaning "Lord and Giver of Life," an encyclical letter with the subtitle, "On the Holy Spirit in the Life of the Church and the World," promulgated by Pope John Paul II on May 18, 1986.

eschatological: of or relating to the end of the world or the events associated with it.

Evangelium Vitae: Latin, meaning "The Gospel of Life," an encyclical letter with the subtitle, "On the Value and Inviolability of Human Life," promulgated by Pope John Paul II on March 25, 1995.

fons vivus, ignis, caritas: a line from the famous hymn, *Veni Creator Spiritus*. Literally translated: "living fountain, fire, love." In English, the hymn books paraphrase: "Thou fount of life, and fire of love."

Gaudete in Domino: Latin, meaning "Rejoice in the Lord," an apostolic exhortation with the subtitle, "On Christian Joy," promulgated by Pope Paul VI on May 9, 1975.

Gaudium et Spes: Latin, meaning "Joy and Hope," a Vatican II document with the subtitle, "Pastoral Constitution on the Church in the Modern World," promulgated on December 7, 1965.

homothymadon: Greek, meaning with one mind; with one purpose.

Lectio divina: Latin, meaning divine reading; holy reading.

Lumen Gentium: Latin, meaning "Light of the Nations," a Vatican II document with the subtitle, "Dogmatic Constitution on the Church," promulgated on November 21, 1964.

Magisterium: The official teaching authority of the church, which has the responsibility to maintain and pass down divine revelation from the written and oral traditions of the church.

metanoia: Greek, meaning the moment of repentance or change of mind.

Mulieris Dignitatem: Latin, meaning "Woman's Dignity," an apostolic letter with the subtitle, "On the Dignity and Vocation of Women," promulgated by Pope John Paul II on August 15, 1988.

Nostra Aetate: Latin, meaning "In Our Age," a Vatican II document with the subtitle, "Declaration on the Relation of the Church to Non-Christian Religions," promulgated on October 28, 1965.

Pastores Dabo Vobis: Latin, meaning "Shepherds I Will Give You," an apostolic exhortation with the subtitle, "On the Formation of Priests," promulgated by Pope John Paul II on March 25, 1992.

Perfectae Caritatis: Latin, meaning "Perfect Charity," a Vatican II document with the subtitle, "Decree on the Adaptation and Renewal of Religious Life," promulgated on October 28, 1965.

pneumatikos: Greek adjective, here used as a noun, meaning a spiritual person.

procatechesis: Greek, meaning first catechism; first teaching.

Protoevangelium: Latin, meaning first gospel or the very first gospel.

Redemptoris Missio: Latin, meaning "Mission of the Redeemer," an encyclical letter with the subtitle, "On the Permanent Validity of the Church's Missionary Mandate," promulgated by Pope John Paul II on December 7, 1990.

Regina Caeli: "Queen of Heaven," the opening words of the Eastertide anthem of the Blessed Virgin, the recitation of which is prescribed in the Roman Breviary from Compline of Holy

Saturday until None of the Saturday after Pentecost. On the occasion of the recitation of this prayer, Pope John Paul II often gave an address to those in attendance.

Sacrosanctum Concilium: Latin, meaning "Sacred Council," a Vatican II document with the subtitle, "Constitution on the Sacred Liturgy," promulgated by Pope Paul VI on December 4, 1963.

synoptic gospels: the first three gospels of the New Testament (Matthew, Mark, and Luke) which present a similar rendering of the gospel.

stichira: a Greek noun for lines, verses.

Theo-foroi: Greek for one who carries God within himself or herself; like *Christo-foroi*. Both terms are actually plural—*all* who carry God or Christ within.

Unitatis Redintegratio: Latin, meaning "Restoration of Unity," a Vatican II document with the subtitle, "Decree on Ecumenism," promulgated on November 21, 1964.

urbi et orbi: Latin, meaning "city and world," a term which signifies that a papal document is addressed not only to the city of Rome but to the entire Catholic world.

Vita Consecrata: Latin, meaning "Consecrated Life," an apostolic exhortation with the subtitle, "On the Consecrated Life and Its Mission in the Church and in the World," promulgated by Pope John Paul II on March 25, 1996.

zebah todah: Hebrew; a common biblical phrase meaning, "sacrifice of thanksgiving."

Bibliography

Benoit, Pierre, O.P.; Leube, Knorad; and Hagolani, Elhanan. *Easter: A Pictorial Pilgrimage.* New York: Abingdon Press, 1969.

Cantalamessa, Raniero. *Easter in the Early Church.* Collegeville, Minnesota: The Liturgical Press, 1993.

Cantalamessa, Raniero. *The Mystery of Easter.* Collegeville, Minnesota: The Liturgical Press, 1993.

Cornelis, H., O.P.; Guillet, J., S.J.; Camelot, Th., O.P.; Genevois, M.A., O.P. *The Resurrection of the Body.* Indiana: Fides Publishers, Inc., 1964.

Gaillard, Dom Jean. *Holy Week and Easter.* Collegeville, Minnesota: The Liturgical Press, 1954.

The Teachings of Pope John Paul II (CD-Rom). Salem, Oregon: Harmony Media, 1998.

John Paul II. *The Theology of the Body: Human Love in the Divine Plan.* Boston: Pauline Books and Media, 1997.

Kreeft, Peter. *Everything You Ever Wanted to Know About Heaven But Never Dreamed of Asking.* San Francisco: Ignatius Press, 1990.

McCann, Dom Justin, M.A. *The Resurrection of the Body.* New York: The Macmillan Company, 1928.

Ray, Stephen K. *Crossing the Tiber.* San Francisco: Ignatius Press, 1997.

Wojtyla, Karol. *Easter Vigil and Other Poems.* New York: Random House, 1979.

About the Authors

Photo by Laurie A. Miller

Jo Garcia-Cobb is a freelance writer who has worked as a journalist in Asia, Europe, and the U.S. She is the author of *John Paul II*, a pictorial biography (Metrobooks, a division of Barnes and Noble, 2000), and coauthor with Keith E. Cobb of *Praying with John Paul II* (The Word Among Us Press, 2006). Keith E. Cobb is pursuing a master's degree in theology at Mount Angel Seminary in St. Benedict, Oregon. Keith, Jo, and their daughter Anna Maria live in Mt. Angel, Oregon.